MY
MOTHER'S
MUSIC

PAUL WEST

VIKING

VIKING
Published by the Penguin Group
Penguin Books USA Inc., 375 Hudson Street,
New York, New York 10014, U.S.A.
Penguin Books Ltd, 27 Wrights Lane,
London W8 5TZ, England
Penguin Books Australia Ltd, Ringwood,
Victoria, Australia
Penguin Books Canada Ltd, 10 Alcorn Avenue,
Toronto, Ontario, Canada M4V 3B2
Penguin Books (N.Z.) Ltd, 182–190 Wairau Road,
Auckland 10, New Zealand

Penguin Books Ltd, Registered Offices:
Harmondsworth, Middlesex, England

First published in 1996 by Viking Penguin,
a division of Penguin Books USA Inc.

10 9 8 7 6 5 4 3 2 1

Portions of this book first appeared in different form in *The Iowa Review* and
Parnassus.

LIBRARY OF CONGRESS CATALOGING IN PUBLICATION DATA
West, Paul, 1930–
  My mother's music / Paul West.
    p. cm.
  ISBN 0–670–86757–8 (alk. paper)
    1. West, Paul, 1930–   —Family. 2. Novelists, American—20th
century—Family relationships. 3. Mothers and sons—United
States—Biography. 4. West, Mildred Noden. I. Title.
PS3573.E8247Z465 1996
813'.54—dc20
[B]   95–43158

This book is printed on acid-free paper.
∞

Printed in the United States of America
Set in Sabon
Designed by Virginia Norey

To
Mildred Noden West
in loving memory

—Do you hate music?

—No, my mother makes me take piano.

—She's right. If you stop now you'll always regret it.

Louis Malle,
Au Revoir, Les Enfants

Contents

My
Mother's
Music

1

‖ A Romantic ‖

Final Sheepskin

Only sister to three brothers, my mother, Mildred, injured herself internally when lifting slabs of beef in 1915. *W. Noden, Family Butcher,* said the sign over her father's shop window, half implying, to my perverse head at least, that Grandfather butchered people by the dozen up the yard in the fly-loud slaughterhouse where I repeatedly humane-killed my four-foot-tall teddy bear in my seventh or eighth year. Entire families volunteered, weary of life, or they dragged victim off-spring, or siblings, amid plaintive screams, across the gravel, the manhole cover, through the green double doors, and roped them by the neck to the thick iron ring set low in the tiled wall. And then they were sausage, needing only to be ground up and stuffed into the emptied intestines of some newly felled beast (you slid one end over a tap and let the water force the increasing swell of the contents all the way to the other end, where it made a discharge gruesome and olive enough to put you off sausages for life).

But I must regain my mother, conscripted into the family business while her brothers won the war. She maneuvered beeves, cut up livers and rumps, and sold them, tendering change—paper or metal—flecked with meat or fat. She delivered too, to outlying homes, with a pony and trap, and on the way (except when the pony bolted) hummed scales integral to her imminent career as a pianoforte virtuoso. Two of her brothers became metallurgists, Douglas dying young in South Africa of a pneumonia brought on by the cold nights of Vereeniging, Transvaal; George becoming rich enough to pollute his liver with best cognac. The other brother, Thurman, became a butcher, mainly out of inertia, perhaps also because he was the only one of the three to go the full bloodshed distance, until wounded, of the so-called Great War. Strangely enough, he died of malnutrition, presided over by an absentminded wife whose errand was to keep him thin. My mother, as she often said, became dogsbody to these three worthies as well as my grandfather's butcher's boy; and even as he, always a soft touch, gave out money and free meat across the glistening pink wood of the counter, and my grandmother mulled her beakers of stout by plunging a red-hot poker into them, my mother slogged away at theory and harmony, short-fingeredly grappled with Liszt at his most obtuse, and took a series of examinations—played, sung, and written—which earned her a thick roll of certificates and culminated in a trip to London for the big ordeal.

I am looking now at her final sheepskin, issued jointly by the Royal Academy of Music and the Royal College ("Patron—His Majesty the King") and signed on February 18,

1915. This final certificate brought my mother to the threshold of half a century's teaching, always to earn money for her parents or her children, and a long way from her dream of concert performances in metropolitan centers, for which she claimed never to have good enough nerves, which I think was just her way of rationalizing the outcome. A performer denied, she sacrificed herself on the less exalted altar of musicological brilliance; never inclined to compose, she would play occasionally for company, or to demonstrate for a pupil, or, in ravishing postlude to a day's teaching, after the crescendo of her last critical foray had ceased. We heard the front door slam, the lock give its congealed crunch; but she did not emerge, and then, at the first notes (of, usually, the *Moonlight* Sonata, the opening Adagio supposed to evoke the lunar-lit shimmer of Lucerne, the lake whose name means "lamp"), my father, sister, and I crept to sit on the stairs outside her door, staring at overcoats on pegs while she cleansed her head of amateurs' fumbles and reconsecrated herself to genius through perfect and stylish execution. She staggered us. After desisting from piano for ten years, she elected to accompany my niece in a series of duos for clarinet and piano, and I heard once again the nimble grandeur of her hands, even as she insisted she was making mistakes. Sight-reading without her glasses, she was perhaps getting a few things wrong, but she covered the flaws with such ingenious brio that it was impossible to tell, especially as the clarinet lagged behind somewhat.

It was music's house, ours: Ludwig's, Franz's, Frédéric's. We others, son and daughter and husband, functioned as subordinate shades to household gods of touch, expressiveness, and panache, to metronome and sustaining pedal. Doing my algebra or French homework in the dead of winter, its clammy gusts whisking my slippered feet with darkness leaked under the door, or during the radiant azure lulls of late summer, when I began schoolwork again with the aroma of harvest in my nose, I heard and felt in and beyond the house a continuum of scales and chords that was proof against all seasons, wars, changes of government or of health, and could be read against the sky like overprinted bedsheets pinned up to air. Even on washdays, when my mother hung linen on the clotheslines, I expected to find it emblazoned with treble or bass clefs from the mere touch of her hands as she set down the "poncher," which squeezed or punched the grime from the fabric into the suds.

After half a century, rheumatism stopped her from playing the way she liked to play, but not from tapping down the five keys (one blue, four white) of her cassette machine, which let her have music wherever she went and especially music she had never played: Delius, Vaughan Williams, Stravinsky, Satie, Copland—composers brought into her ken by the son who, after twenty minutes of her tutelage, quit the brocaded piano stool forever, somehow unable to stomach mother as music teacher. This is odd, as it was she who taught me to read by four years old and, by eleven, some of English grammar, a subject to which she brought the same acumen and exquisite mental discipline as to harmony and counterpoint. By way of tribute to her, on a thousand counts, I draft this memoir in the form of a fugue, I the musical illiterate who listen to symphonic music, Walton to Rubbra, Harris to Sessions, half a dozen hours a day. She always had Roget's *Thesaurus* in hand, as a word-lover would; to her, it was some kind of musical instrument, full of new things to say. In similar fashion I myself keep on thumbing through the current Schwann *Record and Tape Guide* and Virgil Thomson's spiky little primer, *American Music Since 1910.* Words were her avocation just as music is mine, and when we met the daily crossword after lunch, it was an exercise in two-dimensional harmony, a hunt for the tune the black squares hid. Or perhaps those squares still say something as arcane as "The toccata at the beginning of Monteverdi's *Orfeo* is a barbaric flourish of every procurable instrument." While I dithered at these puzzles, she tossed out the very words we needed, having studied her *Thesaurus*, which I had not: *plasma, buffoonery, primula*, without even seeming to think about it. I admired *primula* especially, right off the tip of her mind. The puzzle seen was the puzzle solved.

Her mind, as ever, roamed along staves foreign to me (except for such perverse mnemonics as Every Good Butcher Digests Fat (EGBDF), while mine did linguistic cadenzas, irresponsibly abandoning a word's current import for its historical one (*lewd*) or making one of two (*Bartokkata*). It was marvelous that we could converse with each other at all, never mind the picky sessions in which she grunted with a leaky smile at mistakes made by pianists playing music she knew backward, while I grunted unsmiling at mistakes in aviation movies (a Liberator took off, was shot down as a Maryland, and crashed as a DC-3). She scrutinized all aspirants and denied them tenure, while I, thank my stars, went from probation to approbation in her green-gray eyes. I was finally forgiven for not having made my boyhood's music with her, not at the piano anyway; but we certainly succumbed together to the music of words. I sat at her feet, my shoulder against her leg, and heard her read Tennyson's *Idylls of the King* or Macaulay's *Lays of Ancient Rome*. I no more knew who the king was than I figured ancient Rome, but the soft incantation coming from above sowed a seed that would eventually survive my infatuation, from ten to fourteen, with aeronautical design. The king and the lays waited me out, then claimed me as their own.

Blue Bags of Sugar

My mother was entitled to certain expectations, having made an investment of trouble and pain in the product called son. Having wrenched her womb when heaving beef about, she found herself unable to conceive, which meant of course that the cocoa-butter pessaries and contraceptive manuals (one of them *Married Love*, by the lyrical megalomaniac Marie Stopes) that I found concealed in the back of the handkerchief drawer had been unnecessary all along. After four years of marriage, she underwent several grueling bouts of gynecology until her womb was aimed the right way (my father was hoping she would leave it as it was, I gather). Impregnable at last, whatever *he* thought, she changed from a woman who lost far too much blood into a young matron with too much milk and a breast-reliever in a dark-green box on the top shelf of the pottery cupboard.

Producing an eight-and-a-half-pound boy at thirty-five, then a daughter two years later, she must have felt untrue to certain idols of the tribe, which required early marriage, immediate bearing of children, and nothing in the way of a vocation. My mother's career began at twenty, though, sanctioned by the professors of the best two music institutions in the land, and for ten years she made repeated efforts to light out for forbidden territory. She secured, in secret, a post as a governess in the city of Sheffield, seven miles away, but her parents soon scotched that. She taught grammar and English literature at a small college near the village, but kept none of her pay. She gave music lessons, the first of thousands, and discovered that marriage—more bindingly than rereading Tennyson's *Idylls*, or Longfellow, or Browning—was a means of escape and evasion. A weirdly self-sufficient crypto-aesthete whom music and a set of tennis almost completely fulfilled, she needed an avenue of retreat more than a husband, and in eventually marrying my father she adjusted a childhood friendship into maturer terms. A playmate of all the Noden children, my father merely reconfirmed his status in their clan; that my mother-to-be changed her name to his was just a triviality of bookkeeping. She had escaped, although in fact only from number 7 Market Street to number 17, but my father had clinched his social rise from working-class coal miners to the bottom of the middle embodied in the small tradesman. Besides, he and two of my Noden uncles had played cricket together and fought the war; he was my mother's fourth brother, in effect, and at some almost unverifiable depth he knew *he* had changed *his* name to Noden, and he didn't mind. Years before, as a boy, he had won a rare scholarship to the grammar school at which my Noden uncles were paying pupils; but his parents could not afford his school clothes, or so they said, and he didn't go after all: the first of many denials.

If his gift was for transfer, my mother's had always been to transcend: not only the clamp of her parents' pragmatic love; the skivvying for her brothers; the tilt of her womb; the barely discernible move up Market Street; the choked gamut of what I see as an essentially Victorian girlhood; but also chronic anemia, for which she endured a diet of chopped raw liver; recurrent migraine attacks that lasted several days, hindered her sight, and caused prolonged vomiting; and baldness (at sixteen, after pneumonia, her hair fell out, then regrew as baby hair, so that even at ninety she wasn't gray). In one of my favorite portraits of her, she releases a winning, acute fourteen-year-old smile beneath a pair of keen, delicate eyes and above a jaw of silky, nimble stubbornness. At about this age, she had just gone on the noxious raw-liver diet and her brother George was being suspended in a special corset from ceiling hooks, to remedy curvature of the spine. Fifty years later, because her fingers kept going numb, she wore a whiplash collar to straighten out the nerves in her neck, and this reminded her of George, whose spine had become as straight as she wanted her nerves to be. Numb fingers, she told me, cannot play. And not to play, knowing how good at it she was, always struck her as an offensive waste.

What was her playing like? I have hinted at this already. It was never a mere translation from paper to keyboard, but very much I'll-show-you-all, a bravura feat of performative zeal in which, in her chosen medium, she vented and honed a fearsome amount of nervous energy otherwise channeled into hurling blue bags of sugar at my father's head (she always missed), after which she would storm out of the house, threatening to jump into one of the local dams. Brought back with flashlights from the woods (or just around the corner if not angry enough to go farther afield), she would calm down over a cup of Ovaltine or Horlicks, on which she then blamed her next day's headache. We were living with a Romantic, a woman who was prelude, fugue, and enigma variation all at once; a volcano inside a Dresden shepherdess; a fasces of naked, convulsing nerves enclosed in savory pastry. So if one of us winked wrong, sniggered, or misintoned, the steeplechasing wrath usually reserved for erring music pupils came our way instead, a shower of darts and brickbats, a Ready! Aim! Fire! onslaught of the compleat denouncer, full of looping hysterical crescendos, subdominant threatening asides, tympanic accusations, jangling triangular rebuffs, and a special oral mode which I can only call instrumental speechlessness, an aghast *sostenuto* pout induced by behavior so barbaric—my father's sarcasms, my sister's snatching for a second slice of cake, an unpalmed burp of mine—that no words could fit, but only the plucked, pulsing lips, the eyes in paired roll upward, the hand plastered histrionically against the temple.

My mother was never dull, not even when she calmed for-
midably down after menopause. The recitatives of her indignation were just music of another kind: royal fireworks to the
steady sun of her pianoforte almost nine hours a day (music
lessons from ten to noon, two to four, five to ten or even later),
year in, year out, to keep us clad and fed, and later on to
supplement our scholarships. In fact, in the profoundest sense,
she orchestrated our lives according to some score unseen by
us but grandly signed, and loosely derided by envious igno-
ramuses under the headings of refinement, culture, and gentil-
ity. To her, what was "decent" meant what fitted your gifts,
what fostered and furthered them, what transformed them into
artifacts of will as impersonal in the end as cave paintings or
the medicine wheels of stones on the Canadian prairies, to all
of which your own arrival and passing were incidental: you
were here, or there, as a conduit for the miracle of human
giftedness, and lucky to be thus equipped. None of my university tutors had this synoptic, almost abstract fervor for
keeping the tubes of talent clear, and few of us, all told, are
deficient enough in ego to see ourselves that impersonally. A
woman of spectacular temperament, as aware of her gifts as
of her students' lack of them, my mother nonetheless registers
in my mind's eye with mordant clarity as an example of brilliant nurture—less on personal grounds than in the interests
of mind in general. An orchid who doubled as a gardener, she
kept on whipping every neuron in sight into shape and blew
lovingly into the synapses.

In kindred fashion, she voluptuously inhaled the smell of
fresh-ground (or fresh-pulverized) coffee; periodically took my
sister Sheila to hospital for radium treatment of a winy nevus
on her left hand (the one she writes with); skillfully arranged
flowers on the church altar to mark the anniversaries of Douglas's death in Africa; agreed to wear the steel helmet and pro-

saic armband of an air raid warden in 1940; spent exactly the same amount on each of her two children (a point of parental honor); but refused to play the organ in the village church. A demonstrated harmony comes through, an eclectic and juicy stew of most things undertaken, a few refused. In this genial ordering she joined an openness to experience with integrity on guard, refusing the role of church organist as something betraying the piano and seeking an eminence, locally, she did not need, but taking to her bosom the Norwegian fiancée of dead brother Douglas and suffering her overlong even after, through some predatory quirk of bereavement, the woman fixed her libido on my vulnerable father, to whom a Nordic novelty was manna from Ultima Thule. Or Oslo. He fell. We heard the sounds of it. There were seismic quarrels in the upstairs bathroom, which my sister and I crouched on the stairs (just where we listened to my mother's piano) to hear. The upshot was that either "Auntie" or my mother would leave. My mother stayed, of course, a brisk and mutinous martyr to her children's future. Besides, Mount Everest does not go for a stroll. Perhaps I am imagining it, but after that episode she played piano with retributive force and even more defiant flash: the winner, remaining only on sufferance, with her bag packed.

Or perhaps I do not understand her at all, she who did simple things for complex reasons, whereas I do the reverse. She kept the family together, as the saying goes, because she had gone to enormous pains to create it: an organized withdrawal from what I think of, after a Victorian book entitled *The Girlhood of Shakespeare's Heroines* (all quite imaginary), as the womanhood of Victoria's victims (all of it real). Not altogether strangely, her own mother's name was Victoria too, which brought home to her the twisted legitimacies of a reign so long it seemed almost part of nature itself.

At any rate, my mother had evolved a policy, somewhere between appeasement and stoicism, that created a future for two children, through whom she would live with perky vicariousness, zeroing in on my sister and me as we left adolescence behind, which was when my father began to tune us out as too elaborate a threat, even at a distance. Not that it was all vicarious: my sister, living at home while attending Sheffield University, found my mother not at a sufficient remove from her private life, so she moved into a dorm in town, which my mother began to enjoy visiting impromptu. So Sheila departed for university in another town, wincingly aware that daughters are subject to crackpot protocols that sons usually elude. Neither of us realized it until long after graduation, but we were both in vastly differing ways our mother's satellites, emissaries, fronts, takers of contingency samples, birds launched from an Alcatraz of class, history, and self-denial, yet one full of music too.

I look back with a pang on the twisted chemistry of a mother love that urged us, coaxed us, backed us up nonstop, and so overmotivated us—as if to outdo *Sons and Lovers* and *The Corn Is Green* in one joint upward academic sortie—that we crashed through our respective paper targets like circus riders and caromed on beyond, hardly aware that, already qualified to earn a goodly living, we had become overachievers, obliviously bent on collecting trophies that would enact and augment our mother's holy code of mental or aesthetic transcendence. What she had forgone we retrieved. We found the grail and brought it home, and she roasted it for us and served it amid thick brown gravy with Yorkshire pudding, crisp and eggy, on the side. A fine edge of dementia characterized her in those days as my father went his shamefaced way, muttering thinly about education and how, especially, it was wasted on girls. My mother kept on adjusting us, her

secret weapons, unaware that what she had undertaken was
nothing less than to remedy the absurd. Deprived of her career,
her life, she came up with a twelve-tone system of her own,
so that there could be music where she had thought there
couldn't, and out of the unlikeliest materials. Her purposeful-
ness, then, was innovative, while her tastes only now and then
approached Schoenberg or anyone like him. My sister and I
were extrusions, between fifteen and twenty-five, say, hardly
in possession of some parts of our lives at all: on loan to fu-
turity, pledged to the possible, invested in gumption. We sang
while she played.

My mother's scheme paid off, of course, in our upward mo-
bility (in my own case it was outward as well, to America),
even to the extent of providing Father with something to brag
about at the pub: Two Clever Children, whom he had never,
as she repeatedly told him, in her own caustic version of the
Sermon on the Mount, lifted a finger or coughed up a penny
to help. By then, though, he was cannier, counterpointing her
self-vindications with a Dickensian saw of his own, which
went: "I always knew they'd turn out well," and then back to
his beer, football, horses, his overall Elizabethan style. He
never had a bank account, he left not a penny, he never owned
a house or anything else except a few high-quality chisels. No
wonder my mother, the Promethean Victorian, offspring of
small proprietors, built her mansion in the sky, made her acre-
age mental, her nest harmonic, and her passions proxy.

Supposed to be to my father what she had been to her brothers (and then some), she rebelled; otherwise she would have
had to escape from her escape. On she went, quietly manu-
facturing the heterodox antilife she had thought up and
bending every effort to cope with its unforeseen demands:
hand-making our clothes during the General Strike, when Father could not even find work to walk five miles to, willing as

he was, desperate as he became. She coached us, in whatever
spare time she had; she gave piano lessons during war's blackout in exchange for black market turkeys, ox tongues, and
contraband pounds of butter. We never went short, especially
of her fierce, harrying love, one waft of which fanned the ember of ambition for days and also made you privy to a subtle
evanescence rare in anyone's world, a warmth as if Creation
itself seemed to cotton to and care about you, as if a radiance
had seeped from the matrix to the mother, who thenceforth
became its intermittent mellow agent, asking no percentage,
knowing the horizon was an optical illusion intended for the
children of those who couldn't see beyond. Beyond Earth's
curvature she sensed that of occupied space.

A Miranda

All *that* seems more than a lifetime ago: the frenzied,
mother-inspired haul out of the bottom social class, out of the
near-bottom of the bottom class in grammar school. How
aghast she was when my teachers, after some sort of Little
League Star Chamber meeting, decided her son was one of
those not clever enough to do Latin, not gifted enough to do
Art, and therefore destined for Woodwork, the British equivalent of Shop. My father, the engineer's fitter, breathed with
relief to find his enigmatic son headed back for the paternal
domain after all. For a few years, while I floundered around
without quite foundering, he seemed at ease with me; but then
I confused everyone, except my mother, by recovering my flair
for languages, getting the first 100 percent score in the Latin
exam administered by the local universities, winning a scholarship or two, and disappearing eventually into the satin maw
of Oxford as a fully qualified carpenter. Years later, I won a
painting prize as well, for a collage of mass executions based

on Hungary or Cuba, and my mother nodded with a smile that would have shamed the Ancient of Days. She had known all along that, where there's a will, there is a six-lane highway. I had routed all of her proxy enemies, and for good measure, I could build her a handy letter rack, bookshelf, or footstool, as well as draw the cross-section of an airplane engine, should she ever need it.

With her children reared, educated, gone, she resumed her innocent gentleness, whose meekest component made her seem blithely vulnerable. Always she was less sure of herself than of her role: when I left for Oxford, she almost caved in, certain I would become "hoity-toity," begin to speak with an unbearable plum-in-mouth haughty lithp, and rend the hand that had fed and watered me. And when I left for New York on board the *Mauretania,* she had visions of my being tommy-gunned in the street and knew I would be shipped home in a coffin. Yokel I may have been as I set my first foot on Manhattan, there to spend a definitive and exotic year, but I wasn't exactly a waif; I actually survived, which she believed only when I walked off the *Queen Elizabeth I* onto the pier at Southampton into her arms. Not so long ago she expressed the fear that floods in Pennsylvania would "wash me away," and I realized how small you remain in a mother's eyes and mind, in spite of years, diplomas, badges of rank, books, taxes, narcotics, brushes with death as a wingtip kissed a rising wave of the North Sea or a cockpit canopy ripped off. Somewhere, in the nursery of her brain's eye, my cradle is always warm, my shawl is always aired. She saw how fundamentally helpless we all are, but also what colossal dimensions the mind trumps up, and her lifetime's role, at least as I see it, had been to minister to the truant will in all its backslidings between the last breast-feed and the first giddy lisp of second childhood. The job went on. She kept on keeping an eye on me, half persuaded I'd be ancient before I matured, and determined to see me through, not to let me make an even bigger hash of things.

Visibly, her life amazes me. She asked almost nothing in return except affection, a stream of unexotic picture postcards (which she pasted into albums with the writing side down), some boxes of fancy American soap, and an annual jet-laggy visit. She prospered on a round of cricket and tennis, soap operas and music cassettes. At eighty she ran amok and left the family house of fifty years, took unto herself her first telephone, checkbook, and refrigerator, to assist her into the twentieth century, in which, a Miranda in a maisonette, an unofficial elder of the village, having migrated exactly a mile in four score years, she smiled evenly upon almost everyone, even upon her misbehaving gallbladder. Rereading popular romances by Netta Muskett, Ruby M. Ayres, and Ethel M. Dell, she was a tourist in the continent of her own nostalgia, with the steel springs of her will relaxed and, ever ready to swing into action, her specialized musical mind and the uncanny urban knack with language that flowed from her elegant letters and sat incongruously alongside her doughty, rural nous.

On her weeks away, at the sea with a younger woman friend, she got herself a seat near the hotel band and chatted with the violinists or the bass-player in between numbers, as if stranded in the caricatural shallows of her dream denied. She sold her superbly tuned piano, much as a Chinese slave might doff the wooden cangue from around his neck; she no longer had to play regularly, had only to hear others do it (also for a living), and thus freed from the treadmill with two pedals hear music uncompulsively, as ontology's bouquet, the mind's poignant and most universal bagatelle. Debussy next, she said. Then—what's his name?—*Finzi.* I tremble. Did she give them A or B? Or, as she did when we were very young, tap their hands with a hot teaspoon in facetious, table-mannerly reproof. Mostly, though, she just threatened with a cooling spoon, in whose contours our impish faces elongated as we went upside down, then righted when she made it twist.

Wise passivity: she thrived on it, having quit her various labors, happy to savor the nonbark of a next-door dog; food on which houseflies had not high-stepped as they once did over the food she unhygienically stored on a cool stone slab in a whitewashed section of the coal cellar; the absence of un-wanted wrong music from neighbor radios; the tindery echoes of a traffic-free street; the reflection of her wide windows' muslin curtains in the gray of the TV screen when it was empty. This was the sweetest tune that life had played to her, like "Cherry Ripe" overlaid with "Greensleeves." "I hope," she still could say, though, "you won't sit in pajamas until teatime. It's . . . You do have other clothes." I go to find a shirt, a belt, some slacks; and, even as Debussy begins his test, am thrilled to feel so slovenly and young.

Still in Pajamas

Still in pajamas, having been distracted by a book on an inconspicuous shelf, I ponder her newfound eagerness, her zest, the extra acceleration of her near-sprint walk, and am puzzled. What preserved and constantly revivified her? Some quirk of genes, perhaps, which I shall inherit if I am lucky. Or a limberness of mind and body that rewards, sometimes, the unremitting busyness of a puritan work ethic. Or even the weird negative humility which enabled her to guy her skivvy-ing role (for parents, children, brothers, husband) as "Sam." Who, we would ritually ask her, is Sam? "*I'm* Sam," she'd retort. More bizarrely, she used to let out with the nonsensical exclamation "Sithee, Bill! Ships!" which not only conjured up a nonexistent navy from before the Boer War and an unknown person's informal name, but also aired an old Derbyshire folk imperative for *See thee.*

In fact, between thirty-five and fifty, she resorted to an old Norse dialect vocabulary, which, perhaps, kept her integrity sweet since it encapsulated and vented all the wrongs there could be. *Maddle* meant to confuse and exasperate her (she never applied the verb to anyone else). *Slawm* was to proffer unctuously insincere affection, often with a quasi-erotic caress. *Scranny* she kept for when we drove her clean out of her wits. *Throng* stood for having too much to do, yet not so much as to *jigger* you (which word, often meaning to bless, to her meant inducing catatonic exhaustion). To *wittle* was to worry. *Maungey* meant miserable. And *chavvle,* one of my favorite words from her, meant to cut cake untidily. Can it be that, highly educated as she was in language and music, she shed her troubles by locking them in archaic, provincial idioms? Then they belonged not to her but to other folks, dead and gone, distanced from her by history, or, if living, by class consciousness and an uncouthness in contrast with which her top-drawer well of English undefiled remained as intact as the individual notes from which a symphony is made. I wonder about this because certain common ruralisms she never used at all, such as *roor* (cry), *mardarse* (spoilsport or crybaby), *gennel* (passageway), *snap* (food), and *serry* (the vocative of "sir," equivalent to the Elizabethan word *sirrah*). Such words, apart from *mizzle,* meaning "to go," she despised as vulgar, fit only for folks she dubbed "common." Yet from that same Viking word hoard which is part of my own birthright as a Derbyshire native, she culled the vocabulary of stress and error, a heterocosm of purgative rebuff. As far as I know, she had no out-of-the-way words for when things were going well, which, as they say, speaks volumes. So does the fact that her favorite word had always been *method*. To dismiss someone finally and without mercy, she said. "He has no *method*," uttering the word in oral italics. The main thing in all human activity was to "*shape*," meaning to be decisive and on the *qui vive* creatively speaking.

Her credo was like a Peruvian balsa tree, easy to strip of its bark and straight; but how it worked in everyday use I shall never know. She was always tuning in to something beyond us all, maybe a few revered chords from Beethoven, maybe a fragment from Malory's *Morte d'Arthur*, maybe iceberg memories of which we children had only the merest glimpse: Gerald White, her father's right-hand man, drowned on the flooded golf links while trying to save a sheep; or Uncle Thurman ("Thurrie") slicing through his femoral artery when his butcher knife slipped. Or was she thinking back to an air raid when, as we all four huddled under the kitchen table against the slithering accelerant scream of a bomb that seemed to be coming down the chimney, she said, "If we have to go, we'll go together." During raids she fed us on mutton sandwiches and cocoa, in our little haven under the cellar steps where my sister and I slept on a quilt spread over the big flat box the billiards table had arrived in.

In innumerable ways a private woman, at whose drift we often had to guess, she somehow got across to you the fact that if you were growing up right, you'd intuit what she wouldn't tell. You had to shadowbox your way to Eden, and that was that. Hence the amenity of her silence on the piano stool after playing a sonata, or in later years watching TV tennis on yet another stool, as if trying to live out some *babushka* image filched from who knows where. From Maria Ouspenskaya? Yet what I see her on most is the one-legged stool occupied by men supervising the manufacture of nitroglycerin: if they doze off, they fall over. My mother knew she

must never doze off but sustain tutelary vigil until we were
fledged; and this she did. If I didn't know her better, I might
attribute her enigmatic quality to a cherished vision of the
long-derelict family estate called Blackston Grange, in Lin-
colnshire, near Howarth, the fact of its having been ferreted
out by a pertinacious genealogy-loving cousin. But we were
long into adulthood when Mother first heard about Noden
headstones in the nearby cemetery, including that of our
eighteenth-century ancestor, Sir John Noden, who had "invented" Cheshire cheese and made out of it a fortune, which
his widow squandered. I am glad to be in a family which invented a cheese so crumbly smooth. My mother saw those
headstones as a little girl but had no idea what she was looking at.

The Grange is a weed-smothered ruin, anyway, and no part
of what I fondly call her music—her concordant fusion of
clashing elements—whereas space certainly is. In the impartial
tone of a disaffected emigrant, she said, "Is that where heaven
is?" She believed in heaven, as in her old-age pension, especially as an earned terminus where everything is "nice," but
she kept casting around for guidance, for guarantees. She
knew I looked through telescopes, and she took the trouble to
peer at the Milky Way, that gallus on the night's shoulder, but
only after standing for ten minutes to let her eyes adapt to the
dark. Space to her was neighbor territory, not the fast-receding
edge of the visible universe. Heaven was a caravansary of
sorts, ready for guests, with amenities, a sapient manager, and
a captivating view, perhaps like the Devon Towers Hotel in
Bournemouth.

I keep such thoughts mainly to myself, as reluctant to ex-
press a positive opinion in the absence of evidence as I am

certain that the absence of evidence isn't evidence of absence. She lived in her universe and I in mine. Hers she more or less postponed. Mine I do not. She spoke with easy disdain for the "box" one's cadaver goes into, but only because she knew the end of life cannot be so grotesque, so empty, as to be merely that. Nix? No, her music was Greek, although Polyhymnia's singing and harmony rather than Terpsichore's music and dancing. The reward for a lifetime's toil is bliss. How can I, who know almost nothing, gainsay that? The music made from clashes in the here and now must surely have a better self in the afterlife; no sensible world, she argued, offers approximations to an ideal that cannot exist. That would be cheating. Her Platonism was an ovation to a universe we did not make, and her hankering for heaven created a perfection here on Earth. Approximation, I console myself, implies the near, and all the nears can back one another up without there being an Afar. As with fugue, which is a texture ungovernable by the pedagogic designs of Cherubini's treatise, there are temporary rules that do not decide the pattern of the composition as a whole. I tackle this unleavable theme, this inexhaustible music, with snippets of some motif I cannot know entire. Friends and neighbors would mysteriously leave cabbages, cauliflowers, and potatoes on my mother's doorstep. She and a friend planned to take a helicopter ride to view a new housing development. She always called her friend of several decades, Kath, "Miss Shaw," and Kath always called her "Mrs. West." Formality linked them as nothing else could. They talked for long hours about fireplace finesse: how to brush the dust up right after the coal is on. One of her oldest chums predeceased her, almost a hundred years old: Mrs. Jagger, grandmother to a rock star of whom my mother eventually heard. I even saw my mother attempt a little jig to some tune on the radio and sing along, on another occasion, to an old crooning melody from the 1920s. Then, with a mischievous smirk, she halted herself, both times, and swept imaginary crumbs from her lap, where a glass of ginger wine would soon be resting, to be sipped with small bites at a digestive biscuit held as gently as if it were a wafer of fungus.

2

|| ALBUMS ||

As Camus Said

Childhood is full of headlong lunges from which, if we are lucky, those tending us hold us back. Planting me on her knees as we faced east through the window's net of tiny panes, Mother would clasp her hand against my forehead and push, easing me back from the world into instant sleep, as if newly molten glass had sealed me off. Sometimes she did this to both my sister and me, guarding us with a palm each, as if we were once again organic parts of her body. We gaped at the light visible beneath her hand and passed out. My mother's hands were warm, square, and solid, alive with magic, and tender. They were also scarred and wealed, worn down by housework rather than by arpeggios. For she was a mother above all, whatever else she did.

And now, older than she thought I'd ever live to be, I repeat

that motion of hers, cupping my own forehead to shut the
world out, fend off the leaping light in the finger-thick picture
window, keep myself from going forward into some red-light
district of the mind, doomed to be my own person and nobody
else's, obliged to get on with my work in spite of everything
(work was a holy word to her). My sister and I *belonged* to
her, who thrilled to have us and take upon herself the chore
of raising us, fanning us to white heat, at last removing her
custodial palm and launching us toward Andromeda as newly
thawed-out beloved matter culled from cullions she hardly
knew. We were loved rotten, and she wanted us to know it
from the first, half minded to coax us back, reverse untimely
twins, into the jealous manger of her womb. What came
through over the decades was that, born to any other mother,
we would have been no more than earthenware embryos, having an aftermath to birth certainly but no future, nothing to
look forward to. My father the sperm-bearer sat back, aghast
and exhausted, reattending to the serious things of life, and
she got on with the fostering, more in the mood of a priestess
than of anything traditional. We were special, as agents say of
certain books, and she was blessed. My own birth took place
on a day of blizzard, with my mother's regular doctor lost in
a snowdrift miles away, my emergence supervised by a couple
of brandy-primed amateurs who sank their forceps into my
skull, gifting me with a sizable dent still hidden by hair. There
was something theatrical about that birth, I inheriting from
my mother, out of propaganda or uterine memory, a horror
of snow that afflicts me still. She should have delivered me in
Palm Beach, pink and balmy, where forceps had body heat
and doctors and/or midwives did not have to drive through
snowdrifts to scoop little boys into the world.

You no sooner think you have said it, pinned it down at
long last, than you learn that a mother is an inexhaustible

object of contemplation, to be plumbed neither by fiction nor
by its opposite. What comes into view is always hiding something else you think you needed even to begin. The reverential
act blows up in your face, not because a sibling says, "You've
got it wrong," but because you know you'll never get it right.
Fine-tune the radio to the same frequency month after month,
as I do at home, and something new always crackles from the
speakers. God, as Camus said, is the only exhaustive realist.

I see now that I am honoring my mother's myth, the way
she is her reputation, which among those who knew her is
mighty (as among some who did not). Having set down something, you start again, building upon it, letting yourself float
out to the very tip of responsible memory, where people trying
to say "perpetuate" say "perpetrate" instead and come up
with runic utterance of a friendly sort, such as "the strength
he alludes arriving" (all culled from the recent airwaves). A
car's mahogany dashboard becomes aromatic in the hot sun,
and you fit that aroma into your life, wondering how much
to respond to it. Does it link up to something even more se-
ductive? Could it be the random key to what you want to
remember? Otherwise why are you attending to it so much?
The Birdman of Kennedy Airport drives around scaring off
seagulls by playing a tape of upset gulls or by shooting blanks.
That too comes in, as does, for reasons known only to my
imagination, the sub-Sahara, the so-called breast cancer belt,
where Burkitt's lymphoma lurks. Are these things I wanted to
mention to my mother, or are they things she already knew
without my saying? Open-minded humans merge into context
without apology or explanation, and you have to hunt them
down, lurking at Kennedy airport or in the sub-Sahara. I
worry that, in trying to be exact about my mother, I have
pinned her down too much, given her a rigid idiosyncrasy instead of a nimble uniqueness.

One cannot make memory obey, or even behave, but one has to suck up to it, pleading and hoping that something salient will come through. Yes, it says, don't you recall how kisses on the tummy evoke asterisks imprinted on the brow of a horse? But you have lost the connection, and it is going to dog you to the end of your days. A lost analogy is two universes wounded. Or so I sometimes think in recovering my mother's complex, lively manner, her pell-mell profundity, her gentle enormity. I could go on, packing words into the gap, but she has to be recovered in action, drawn in through the mind of an infant like mercury through a pipette. Is she there? Can I bring into use the child I was, with a hole in my forehead from where the handlebar of my tricycle went in when I fell off? *Him?* Why, he is more gone than she. I knew her better than I ever knew me, yet it is through little me I have to tease out the young mother she was, like some bulkstar.

Snapshots

In one treasured photograph, I am perhaps a year and a half, on top of my head a huge ascending quiff of sun-burnished curls that form also down the back of my neck. I have a thick tan and am sitting on the beach with the aghast mutinous look of someone who has gone in his india-rubber pants. Between my hands I am fashioning a sand pie and have reached a crisis, imploring the heroic picture-taker for help. Seated behind me, my mother has a world-weary look, reaching to the top of her scalp as if to quell a headache. Looking out to sea, with her back against the wall, she wears the confident, unimpeachable look of a pregnant young mother, solidly into her thirties. Not quite buxom, she has the small hands of all our family, and her eyes are taut in the act of closing. She has had enough, which is no doubt what her upturned summer cloche signifies atop its bollard: a chamber pot or war helmet. My father's suit jacket covers an entire corner of the seat, robust and filled as if a dwarf has hidden within. Clearly my father has asked her to smile and the requisite effort has stunted a daydream, cut it short, and she is not going to oblige. Her face is *her* face, after all; why embellish it when it will be black and white? All her life, my cooperative mother nonetheless posed such awkward questions, never finding it enough that her next role, say, is to shove the push-chair with her child in it, lordlike riding. And of course the accursed sun is blinding, which is why that plump-faced little boy five yards in front of her has mounted a scowl announcing: *Move the glare, please, I can't see past it. I'm scared.* Brown little grub, he is going to crack any minute and run back to her next the seawall. It is too hot for them all three that day in 1931, and the idyll has moldered, fabulous but flawed, there in Bridlington or Cleethorpes on the east coast of England, where the water makes your teeth chatter.

I linger on this scene because in it I discern for the first time the worried, harassed look I wore until my teens, when I smoothed out and cheered up. As a child I resembled the first infant Marxist or someone who had just read all of Schopenhauer. Not a cheerful kid, I had a problem with bright light and could have been suffering from first migraines (the blight that dogged me until, far too late, I went on propranolol). I was always squinting, perhaps afraid that the sun kept following me around, as the child psychologist Piaget said most children thought it did. There my mother lounges, with one out, one to go, committed to maternity and incessant worry, once again harnessed distraught to the implacable engine of life, hearing herself play Chopin for sheer emotive pleasure. She looks rumpled as a milk-sour bib. And her boy is a rumpled little blob too, his big head daring the rays to singe him, turn that corkscrew hair to straw while he pouts fatherward, watching Daddy's dickey bird.

Not much later, I am swinging along the promenade, left hand in my mother's. Another seaside picture (nobody took pictures inland, it seems, so all photographs of that era came from August, once annually). My scowl is in place, though more purposive than before, and my right hand holds some kind of trophy. Clearly I have retreated from an unsuccessful sand castle or am going to try again, all pique and ambition. I look so limber my joints seem loose, and I am already some-what pigeon-toed, making me reel away from my mother only to be reeled in again. The swarming curls have been brush-bashed backward and I have an almost human look, coiffed and smooth. My mother's expression is that of good-natured autonomy, a very young nubile thirty-seven. In one hand she bears a sharp-cornered suitcase holding, perhaps, a teapot and tin cups, so where did the hot water come from? No, there was a bottle of Tizer in it, brown fizzy sweet with a ruddy rubber ring in the screw top to keep the air in tight. My stride is too long, I am looking down, and I have a small yacht under my arm. This was going to be a serious day. A bucket dangles from our conjoined hands. We are walking with a mission in mind, perhaps to the local park in Blackpool. My sister is nowhere in sight, so how is my father working the camera with a baby to manage? Perhaps there is no sister. I get the elastic sense that the two years dividing our births last five: there was a companionless gulf in which time, with brawny obsequiousness, let me revel in myself or let me think I did.

Just look at that hugely preoccupied boy, who already has a slight tummy; he has an ultrahuman look, an air of unjudged alienation. No doubt he is thinking years ahead, while his mother, thrilled to have him, weary of being with him, wishes he were smaller, lighter, able at least to spell her with the little suitcase. But look closely: he is holding the bucket and she his wrist. Is it the yacht that troubles her, then? Or just being photographed? She is chatting to him without looking at him, but his lips twist down into a coral smidgen and his left temple bulges close to where his tricycle gouged him. I am not happy to have been this lad. Whenever I look at him, he seems rattled, put off, waiting for the ax to fall. Now I see it: burned and bronzed, he has been in the sun all day, and though weary he doesn't want to quit, but he is having to, driven forward by that maternal wrist-clasp. She, the devotee of Victorian poetry and Romantic music, is out on her feet (jiggered, almost scranny, as she would say) and craving a nap, while her puzzled, defiant boy wipes the salt from his newly baptized yacht, pronounced with a German rasp. I dote on that face of hers, its smile suppressed by tolerant indignation. She looks eighteen, but, I find as I enlarge Xeroxes of this shot, the incipient smile of her opened mouth deepens and blurs to that of someone breathing hard, and her expression changes from cautious euphoria to one of forbearing exhaustion. With my mother, you know which one it is, and this young jackanapes to her right has sensed it, recognizing she is no longer *for him* that day and is tugging him homeward, hence his long light-heeled gait, the twist in both ankles as he tries to gain some footing. Strakes help a jet plane fly sideways, so maybe that's what he's doing. He is going home at an angle, not so much home as a boardinghouse or private hotel whose owners marvel at the visitors, wondering why they make this ugly pilgrimage once a year, with the ocean too cold to bathe in, the accommodation inferior to what they came from. Less private anyway. The answer is fresh air: they come for the bristling wind to clear their noses.

What a svelte figure my mother has. She might be a young immigrant arriving at Ellis Island, aimed for the clinic where they test your eyes with a buttonhook. She might have come from Poland somewhere, with this disgruntled child to tend her in afteryears. She looks generous, resilient, neat. Who would not want her? Only the boy with the *Yachtung,* as we sometimes said it, being slick. My mother is Mother Courage, peering down the busy street at the remainder of her life. If only, she'd say, it had been New York or Athens, meaning New York, N.Y., and Athens, Greece.

In another photograph, which became the authoritative baby picture, I brim with good temper, almost smiling. I am three, chubby, approachable, clear-eyed, and flanked by a baby sister in a nightdress, whereas I am wearing a woolen suit. This was my mother's favorite snap of us, carefully posed as we were on a music stool. The picture emphasized the good humor she expected of us (and we of her), as if photographs committed you to anything behavioral. How she leeched the scowl out of me I have no idea, but perhaps I was a sucker for attention and being well lit in a studio full of bear rugs. It was more like an *occasion,* whereas casual snaps were inconsiderate breaches of one's privacy. My mother went to some length to create a wholesome record of our early lives. My father smoked his pipe more often than he otherwise would, adding stability to the scene because, so the myth went, everyone trusts a pipe smoker. Like Stalin, I suppose. At any rate, my mother got her heart's wish in this staged photograph, and it sat for many years on her piano top as an icon even if, under those studio lights, our arms and faces had the glabrous look of diabetics' toes, pallid and shiny. It was the old familiar yearning of the mother that trapped us: my mother wanted us never to grow up, and perhaps this photograph could freeze time's arrow, corralling us inside a gilt frame, a professional shutterbug's sepia tint. She had locked her beloveds in a time machine, gifted them with only the one superlative mood, set the twain side by side on that stool in a didactic pose of eternal good-natured togetherness, not siblings but an altar boy and an altar girl.

Later on, I began to see what fascinated my mother and kept her teaching music. She wondered where evil came from, and why, and in this minor instance bad temper, cross looks, intemperate behavior. In that she was Wordsworthian, having seen how as tots we trailed clouds of glory from us, idyllic little passengers that we were. Why did we go bad? Because the world was bad? Then why was the world bad? Was she inching her way toward a belief in Satan? I never knew, but I was aware she had read her Milton, certainly *Paradise Lost*, and had pondered in detail the facts of the so-called Great War. Surely babies, never mind how full of selfish genes, did not spawn evil of their own accord. Evil came floating in to the planet as part of some malign panspermia. It never occurred to her that evil might come from evolution's twitch, from some haphazard mix of impulses: an unfortunate by-product from a process that yielded something good as well.

My scowl or frown bothered her, then, suggesting I was a less than Wordsworthian child, who would go on to use foul language and get universally into trouble—a rough boy who punched girls. She was right. I cared as much about decorous behavior then as I do now about what's politically correct. I am afraid I belong to those who cannot resist a verbal opportunity, whatever the cost; the unique, coruscating phrase draws us on and in, much like the eternal feminine Goethe lauded. One word I uttered, picked up from the village street, was *bugger,* and this upset all who heard it, not that they linked it to buggery or Bulgaria. It was full-fledged taboo, especially in the homes of the well-to-do, relegated to use by the poor, which of course we were. My first *bugger* I said at my paternal grandmother's (they were even poorer than we were; God bless their roast-beef sandwiches), and I was at once, as it were, slammed shut, forbidden to say anything more that day. I recognized the ineffable power of the word, never mind which one; this was authentic magic, and I dimly resolved to avail myself of it in the life to come and the next life too.

Other Anglo-Saxon monosyllables came my way as well, mouthed in the toilet or under the sheets at night, heirlooms from a race of warrior-tosspots long wiped out, along with Queen Boudica (as the Romans called Boadicea), yet part of my heritage all the same. Tiny as I was, I enjoyed the sound of certain words, crude and percussive, but of course did not hear hundreds of other words at all until much later. Had I done so, I would have been too overjoyed to attend to my teachers at all. Yet this was far from being my mother's fault: before I was ten, I had heard, at her knee, such enigmatic, fog-laden words as *grammar, rhyme,* and *clause.* I have no idea why, except that my mother was force-feeding me against the next disaster. A boy who knew the word *grammar* (without actually knowing grammar itself) would not even hear the *bugger*s of this world; he would be too busy treating his mind to the word's implications and its beautiful ancestry. My mother was not so much a highbrow as high-toned. Although she was not quite willing to admit that culture was what the people do—*anything* they do—she did have a countrywoman's earthy practicality; but to her, you could be down to earth without becoming sordid. What if gaffer Wordsworth, as his locals called *him,* had used swear words? I am sure he did. What would she make of that? Trailing clouds of profanity, Mother? Inescapable contact with the common herd, she'd say, inevitable outside nunneries and monasteries. Yet, when TV came along, she loved the wrestling and the six-gun killings in the cowboy movies. She was complex enough to write a book about.

To keep us within view while she was pinning out washing on several clotheslines that ran from the house to a neighbor building, then back to a post, she put me as an infant in a big linen basket, almost a coracle in shape, made of bright bamboo and large enough for two babies. Here, no doubt, I fantasized, at least until my sister arrived, and then there were indeed two in the basket. I tried to examine my sister's gorgeous blue eyes, and then to pry them out of their sockets. Next thing, there were two laundry baskets, somewhat apart, with a child in each, murmuring and burbling. Surely I have time-slid backward here, but the imposing events seem later than they were. I have no exact chronology between being an infant (infancy means having no speech) and being a four-year-old who can read and has some weird words (of all kinds) in his hoard. I knew this, though, thanks to my savant of a mother: those who did not read were missing a whole continent of life, as open as a skylight to anyone who could tilt a wrist and find a page. This was a given in our household. My father, when he had work, stayed up all night in order to read, regularly going without sleep, as he had always done during the Depression, when he had no work for as long as a year. When the industrial-military complex failed, he stepped sideways into the stealthy world of books, which excited him as gambling did, but cost less. In our house a book was holy, as was a piano and a little cardboard case of geometrical instruments—compasses, divider, protractor, set square, and such. There was no limit to the mind's power: this was the lesson we learned at all points. The true miracle was within, not on the altar or at the bank. Mind was the marvel, and don't you forget it, young you. I didn't, though, confronted with the material riches of this planet, I often questioned it. My mother kept me straight, like some pirate of the spirit, some buccaneer of the book, and all else—fresh-ground coffee, even chocolate cake, a new pair of creaky shoes—was dross. What a magnificent bigotry that was.

3

AT THE MOVIES

In the Shilling Seats

Having lost an eye in the war, my father was never much for going to the picture show, but my mother and I went regularly, sometimes bolting meals to get there on time. In an adult's care, I got to see A(dult) pictures as well as U(nrestricted),* so going to the flicks with Mother was a bonus on top of the thrillers I saw at Saturday afternoon matinees (*The Thunder Riders*, Buck Jones and Ken Maynard, Gene Autry and Tom Mix, *The Clutching Hand*—I would walk home, not far, from the Electra with my hand forked into two tubers, waggling it erratically up and down to mimic the main character's palsy). My mother did no such thing, of course, nor did she mimic Doris Day, one of her favorites besides Ava

---

* There was another category: H for Horror or Horrific.

Gardner. She was as omnivorous as I, and resented it not at all when people, seeing her at the movies so often, teased her for violent and vulgar tastes. According to them, a high-toned music teacher from a well-to-do family should not be mingling with the proletariat at their breads and circuses. She and I were escapists, she from a compulsory labor force started by her mother, I from bullying. So for a few hours we lived among Curtiss biplane dive bombers painted gaudy colors, with their wheels retracted into the nose, and innocuous comedies in which Doris Day, Miss Rheingold writ large, made everyone feel virtuous for liking someone so wholesome. We paid, then walked up the slight incline to the Bobs and the Nines (the shilling and ninepenny seats), heedless of bursting banging paper bags, catcalls, wolf whistles, balls of paper curving in flight above the patrons, and, as the lights dimmed, the pink fantastic screams of goosed girls, the pungent shower of bits of orange peel flung through the projector's long fan of light. With a roar of unappeased hunger, the crowd settled down to their standard cries, depending on the movie's type: "He's *behind* you" for thrillers, "*Nice* tart" for Doris Day. There was never silence, so in a way the movies *were* partly silent, which gave them a nostalgic feel, especially for my mother, who had grown up on movies augmented by an organ or a piano, with all dialogue printed on the screen. Smeg, the usher (his real name Smedley but humiliatingly shortened as if it had been Smegma), walked the aisles with a big flashlight, and kept the peace by cuffing whisperers and bashing callers on the head. No one answered him back. Sometimes he hauled hecklers from their seats and bundled them outside, fatally giving others a chance to ram a compost of peanut bags, apple cores, and lollipop sticks down the shirt collar of the person in front. My mother and I took our aesthetic pleasures amid a sea of hooligans. Often, as we walked in and up, I wondered at the fate of the less than able-bodied in that auditorium: the woman with the iron foot, who smelled so bad that dozens moved away when she sat down; Reggie Jessup, the spastic shoemaker, who, in order to hit a nail, aimed away from it (I had seen this time and again, fascinated, at his shop); the blind, the deaf, the otherwise halt, all drawn helplessly to this pleasure palace of misbehavior and third-rate Americana. The patrons were always on the move, youths with their flies open, girls with lips sealed on a mouthful of something or other, cripples with chronic cramp, babies throwing up into their mothers' arms, and dogs chasing one another, to bite or couple among the watchers' legs. More than vivid, at least to imminently erotic me, were the sisters Ella, Della, and Bella, who walked in three abreast with arms linked, their long legs poised like oiled pistons above six-inch stiletto heels, their huge cloned bosoms undulating as they walked, their eyes aimed into the little bright meatus of the all but hidden projector awaiting them.

My mother and I sat hand in hand, stiltedly demure, from our first show to the last, a couple of primitives plugged into a more colorful world, vaguely aware that this was *art* of a kind, cheap and ephemeral, yet visual chocolate. Twisted-up silver paper flew all about us, in exquisite arcs, and the stench of fruity bubble gum rose and settled to a rhythm of incessant smacking. This being England, there was no popcorn, but a young woman in uniform tried to sell ice cream during the interval, jostled and pinched. Of course there was smoke as well, assuming all the types of cloud formation as it rolled and curled through the shaft of light that one day would remind me of an earthy Plato. The folk who ran this cinema were Belgians, refugees from my father's war, their name Gée, which caused them no end of sentences beginning "Gee whiz," but I, learning French, decided their name should be said

Zhay. The *Zhays* had a quiet, humiliated, greasy look, having come from one orgy of fried food to another. It must have seemed just like home when they found they had emigrated to a village with two fish and chip shops, and the nightly reek of vinegar and hot fat that wafted down the main street must have helped them no end.

I remember less the movies we saw than the cries that interrupted them, most of all the general-purpose "Eigh-up," meaning "hello," "bugger you," and "look at me" all in one. Many cries were just bleats or roars; their emitters had come here to make a noise, and they found themselves answered with cries deafening and coarse. One or two times, my mother and I, afflicted with atavistic temptation, let forth uncouth cries of our own in the darkness, interrogating the answerers, answering the interrogators, but achieving only vocal tinsel against the mighty outbursts of testosterone that echoed off the slate walls of the movie zoo. There we sat, mostly aloof, testing our concentration, gently flicking off our faces drops of wet that sometimes landed, down from the ceiling or horizontally along the row we sat in. You had to put up with a lot for your shilling, but if you kept your mind on the task at hand it wasn't too bad. Smeg walked about, a demon in the darkness "tatting" the hobgoblins who pleased him least, which was to say flicking their earlobes with middle finger released abruptly from the tip of his thumb. Sometimes in his cups, he mumbled nightly runes, thickly and delightedly saying with intrusive lambdacism (almost a dialect): "I like them big *tlabs!*" I like those big ears. How fast a lisp came on him. Perhaps that was the way he thought God spoke. We saw him sidling about under the rosy exit lights and nodded to each other. Smeg was on duty, and all was well. Besides, boys with their mothers he never tatted. This was where Mother and I loved to be, gobbling our mints and chocolates with mindless abandon, then laying the packets beneath us with practiced stealth.

When the show ended, the two of us sat still, the better to observe the departing horde, purged and weary but still fit for a squabble outside on the way to the pubs. Once they had cleared the aisles, some of them bundling past us with an ungracious thank-you, the halt and the maimed took their leave, reeling and grasping at the seats. My mother told me it was rude to stare, but I stared anyway, watching them out of sight with the muted frenzy of a born collector. What they went to, God only knew: a bed made of fried bread, a sink full of leeches, a cupboard full of wooden legs infested with termites, a ceiling that bosomed low above them from the weight of urine in the room above. Now the lights were up all the way, and the cleaners arrived as we departed, two women with their hair in curlers, a cheap cigarette drooping from the bottom lip (Woodbine or Park Drive), and huge bubbles of conjunctivitis at the corners of their eyes, formed on the dust they stirred up. Ethel and Annie, I think, nightly contending with an army that unloaded itself and moved on. I stared at Ethel and Annie too, wanting their secret, wondering if they had chocolate bars cached in their knickers for afterward. Then we were out in the rain or the snow or the sooty-smelling heat, hand in hand walking home to two people who had no idea what we'd seen and never asked.

Evening Becomes Electra

My memories of our movies are not as dependable as I would like. Clear in the beginning, from 1937 to 1939, they blur as war breaks out in September of the latter year, then clear again as the "phony" war brings only slight changes in daily routine (gas masks and air raid siren drills). Then, for a while, as Nazi bombers with their wobbly drone come over nightly and the cinema closes, I go to the movies in my own memory at exactly six o'clock: movie time. The bombers come over just as I am going to sleep, about nine, with my sister, on a makeshift bed in the cellar. Then, as Hitler turns his bombers' attention elsewhere, the movies return, the same ones as before. There is scant room in transatlantic convoys for reels of film intended for my mother and me, who talk about our favorites incessantly without, however, fixing them in our minds for years to come. The price of seats went up, but there was always ice cream or Popsicles halfway through the show. We took our own candies, though, using ration coupons—everything was scarce. I began to believe that, without oral supplement from the audience, the movie reels would cease to spin. No chew, no show. What can the connection be? Does visual concentration require the wiping out of other senses in some such mindless act as chewing? If so, what of the ears? Does the sound of chaw blur them so much they find all that's said and half heard acceptable, consonant with the seen? My ponderings about the movies never got too far: I succumbed to nonstop chromatic aberration, at about fourteen saying to my mother as we walked home after yet another show:

"In America they call them movies, not films. Fillums. Like the heebie-jeebies."

"Something familiar made diminutive," she said, shooting a little above my head.

"Come again, Mommy," I said. "Is that why?"

"I don't see why it shouldn't be."

She had defined it as if it had been sonata form. That was the way her mind worked, snapping the subject shut like a trap. So I memorized what I almost understood (isn't that the gist of learning?) and filed it for later reference during some hell-sent examination—I might use it to distract the examiners from my basic ignorance, my inability to calculate baths draining and filling, monkeys ascending greasy poles at the rate of three feet a day but losing a foot every twenty-two and a half hours. A movie flicked its tail; that was it. It was a pet, a tot, a misbehaving infant. We would never catch ourselves saying art-ie—unless it was Artie Shaw—or the sculpturies, the novelies, the poemies. This was a plural art form on its own, requiring only that you were not blind. You cozied up to it, offering little, hardly being demanded of, and had a dream for sixpence. Books cost about the same back then, but they demanded a great deal, except from such masochistic little freaks as me, who in a gray-silver notebook wrote down all the words I found I didn't know. I still have it and have forgotten what some of the words mean, though I remember at random *opsimath* and *heteroclite*. Such terms never afflicted the movies or (to put it another way, less patronizing) the art of film.

What about musics, plural, then? My mother suggested all art was music of a sort. Music was the supreme one. I had come across something like that in one of my textbooks, about all art aspiring to the condition of music. I saw. Music was the toughest of the lot: a foreign language not in the least representational. Its only "meanings" were through iterative association. I have a dreadful feeling that, under my mother's expert tutelage, sentences I began at ten I finished off only at fifteen. Or left them dangling, like a Nazi parachutist in an unpublished (never shown) novel of mine, whom I abandoned in mid-page (357) and never went back to. There was something about movies I couldn't pin down. It was what America cared about most of all, even more than about jazz and swing; and yet, I thought much later—again only the other day, in fact—why did Orson Welles's movies get so lousy a press in his home country? Even such a marvel as *Chimes at Midnight*, butchered by long-forgotten Bosley Crowther? That movie was art, but they skewered it for not being democratic. I would love to hash these matters over with my mother, wondering aloud with her why America cares little about literature and serious music, always touting movies and moviedom, never a new novel or a new symphony. When was a serious novel or a symphony last mentioned on the TV news? Is money the answer, or is it something far more deeply interfused? Cant, bigotry, hate? Machismo? I have never begun to figure it out; my ten-year-old unease at the phrase "the movies" has never quite died down, evoking H. G. Wells's *The Time Machine* and Queeg's mindless jiggling of ball bearings in *The Caine Mutiny*. We ride the movie forward, leading with our chin. The perfect movie is one with no dialogue at all, either printed or spoken, thus recapturing for us the bedrock mysteriousness of life, its arrogant ephemera, its loutish vicissitudes.

Such notions, in crude gesticulatory form, began in the wartime moviegoing my mother and I never apologized for. We shared the movies as we would never be able to share music, passionate as we both were about it. The moviegoing of those early years became a hallowed gallery for me, in which being alone with my mother was as important as watching the screen. Listening to her play the piano was quite different: I started at a vast disadvantage, whereas at the Electra—what a name to find in a mining village!—we were even-steven as the opening credits crawled. Callow as I was, I was a genuine companion to my mother (or so I thought), not a merely appended kid. What we saw was secret stuff, American, and depended on a different lifestyle from that of the village. So began my desire to visit America and test it out against its movies. Was it a bigger arena than my notion of Curtiss dive bombers and swing bands suggested? Did everybody have a tan? Were the cars actually yellow, red, purple, orange? Did each home have a separate post box on a stake right out in the open for anyone to steal from? Was there constant shooting? These greenhorn yearnings more or less matured under the guidance of Americans I met later on: Lynn Bartlett, Donald Hall, Ernest Hofer, Glenn Maddy, Wilfrid Sheed, Bud Stanton, and John Walsh, all correcting my worm's-eye view and steering me westward.

You see, I have surrendered to impetus, lost my mother, and skipped a dozen years. The recoverer of memory has to nail his feet to the ground, reminding himself that memory—which brews an ecstasy and whips up a heedless wind—has to be put on Pause as often as you can. It moves at the speed of a UFO and with similar whim. If you are lucky, salient events string themselves out along a line like Christmas lights; if you are not, you will be hacking through tree rings with your first memory, the one you wish to start with at the core. If love is a religion with a fallible god, is not memory a god with a fallible religion?

How amazing, after all that, to find the movies of one's childhood showing up at two in the New York morning, scratchy, muzzled-sounding, and unheralded, although often honored in the movie guides. My mother and I, a phantom duo, walk into the Electra all over again as the huge feral cries of miners rise and then merge into the insistent one of "Why are we waiting?" The movies never started on time, so the screen itself took a host of hits from bottles and hard-boiled candy (known locally as "spice"), giving it a messy patina. Once again *One of Our Aircraft Is Missing*, *The First of the Few*, and *Orchestra Wives* enliven and sadden me. At these movies I am alone, though rich with handheld memories and the aftertaste of chocolate raisins. Heroic propaganda, the first two have aesthetic merit, allow time for the pensive, even though the second one has now become *Spitfire*. If you were a Basie or a Woody Herman fan, there was too much Glenn Miller in *Orchestra Wives*, in spite of "At Last," "Serenade in Blue," and "I've Got a Girl in Kalamazoo," tunes at which my mother sniffed, enduring them because this was the movies we were at, and lines such as "This life" (of an orchestra wife) "is as glamorous as a gymnasium." *Orchestra Wives* is full of featherhead prattle, yet it gives me a pang always.

All three of these movies come from 1942 and so stand as emblems of the Blitz, two of them well-bred tableaux, one a sappy story with a big band like an insurance policy behind it. *Wives* also brings back for me *Sun Valley Serenade* of the year before, again with Glenn Miller, which was why, when I began to collect records, I rarely picked up Miller, not even "In the Mood" and "Chattanooga Choo-Choo," both from that movie. My mother enjoyed the heroics of the downed Wellington bomber and the quiet tweed jacket of R. J. Mitchell, the dying Spitfire designer played by Leslie Howard, whom she admired. The orchestra movies passed by her almost unnoticed, but not, in *One of Our Aircraft . . .* , the echo of the BBC radio announcer—Frank Phillips or Alvar Liddell or John Snagge—who would gravely explain in a refinedly antiseptic voice, "One" (or more) "of our aircraft is [are] missing." In those days of war, the hitherto anonymous announcers at the BBC gave their names, as if to encourage, to soften the blow of constant bad news. How did it go? "Here is the six o'clock news, and this is Frank Phillips reading it." How blunt. My mother liked Frank Phillips and Alvar Liddell best, and we often imagined what they looked like, these distributors of grief, only to gasp in amazement when their photographs finally appeared, not at their severe suits and ties, but at how like everybody else they looked. You could just see them in their gardens—allotments, as we called them then—or opening an umbrella. Myself, I thought the harbingers of horror should look a shade more Faustian, a word I had not then acquired, or Frankensteinian, a word I had hewn from *Frankenstein Meets the Wolf Man* (1943), another of my staple standbys. My mother liked this too, but never made the error we small boys did of calling the so-called monster Frankenstein. We were at all costs monster-oriented and approved of Wolf Man Chaney, Jr., and we didn't care that this was the only time Bela Lugosi played the Monster. His very name, whispered in class, or into the ear of a boy about to be tortured with dead birds' beaks, was enough to create a shudder. Nothing frightened my mother, though; after all, she was a butcher's daughter; as the rhyme said, "the ugliest shop in the street."

I belong to the fast-diminishing band of those who know how *One of Our Aircraft Is Missing* got its name, and I imagine what the response nowadays would be if the title had been—lifted from the saddest broadcasts during the Battle of Britain—*Ninety-one of Our Aircraft Are Missing*, say. More uplift came from the echo of Winston Churchill's famous speech about the same battle, in which he lauded the "the first of the few." That romantic, honorable salience has gone now, and *Spitfire* the movie gets mixed up, especially in video parlors, with another of the same name, a Katharine Hepburn melodrama in which she plays what used to be called a tomboy.

My mother and I sank our teeth into the honor, the epic, the heroic formulae, with an emancipated bit of our brains marveling that the British were still making movies amid the bombs. Yet, truly, all they had to do was open the door and film the appalling devastation going on nightly: London and the provinces on fire, with bombs aimed into the fires again and again. Riding to school on my bicycle at eight o'clock each morning, going north, I saw the sun coming up in front of me, in the wrong place. It was the steel city of Sheffield, blazing on the horizon seven miles away. "Don't look," I recall my mother's saying. There were thousands of people melting in the blaze. It was saner to try to conjure up before me, as I pedaled, scenes from *One of Our Aircraft* . . . (Godfrey Tearle playing the utter gentleman with Dutch schoolteacher Pamela Brown) or David Niven talking to dead Mitchell in the clouds as a Spitfire roars over: "They can't take the Spits, Mitch, they can't take 'em." Not bad as something to hold on to while cycling in the direction of carnage. I even pretended, on board my bike, to be a Spitfire pilot racing to the rescue northward, to get the people out just in time and then shoot down the Heinkels with a curt ring of my bell. No, they couldn't take the Spits, Mitch, never. My mother understood how schizophrenic one had to be, with the war raging but the protocols of peace there to be observed: sausages, movies, piano lessons, algebra, the nervous blinking for which she dosed me regularly with quinine and phosphoric acid. Was I blinking because of the war, the tumult I found just past the edge of everything? I had an almost surreptitious childhood, full of toys, lamb and beet in an age of food rationing, daily pulp fiction to read, movies to goggle at, and fragile 78s to play on an ancient junked record player retrieved from a scrap heap and in which, out of perversity, I had mounted a thorn instead of a needle. It almost worked. Then I discovered that, because metal was scarce, someone had actually invented a plastic needle, almost identical with my thorn. I had just missed making a fortune out of something I might have patented. There was still hope, even if I never improved at math. My mother watched my fumblings with concern, knowing there were better things than boyish ones, if only she could tune me in to them.

Exquisitely spoken Frank Phillips designed the Spitfire, choking blood onto his blueprints, while Alvar Liddell, bandleader in a long white tuxedo, carried a bomb in his trombone case right into Hitler's headquarters and then, after the explosion, made his way home through Holland, led by Googie Withers and Godfrey Tearle. Not one of them uttered a curse word, not even Hitler, and only Glenn Miller died, victim as I later learned of an RAF bomber pilot who salvoed his bombs over the English Channel right on top of the Norseman in which Miller was flying to Paris. I hoped they would keep the Count, the Duke, Benny, Artie, Woody, Harry, Gene, and Tommy in America, where they belonged. With RAF pilots that careless, you could get killed even while riding to school in a false dawn.

No One Ever Said Africa

My mother had prevailed over my father in the matter of my name. The one I bear was the one she truly wanted, though my father thought it sissified, but less so than another of her favorites, Carl. What did my father want to call me? He had no idea, but I think he preferred a military number, like the one I eventually acquired: 503524. My second given name, Noden, which means "guardian of the abyss" in Norse folklore, was my mother's maiden name, a rare one indeed; I have often wondered what my well-read mother made of it, and how "Noden" got into Norfolk, where her father came from. How had she hit on Carl? Why not Saul, a form of Paul? And, if she knew nothing about the abyss and its guardian, did she know that Paul meant "small" in Latin? I have always looked for Nodens in the phone books of my travels: one in Pittsburgh, one in Ithaca, New York, but I have never looked up the name's bearers. I am a watcher of planes rather than a seeker-out of distant relatives. I am happy nonetheless to have my mother's surname embedded in mine, just as happy to have a name short enough to be printed horizontally across the spine of a book.

Anyway, young Paul grew a mop of honey-golden curls that my father found as sissified as my name; but my mother refused to have me shorn, at least until I was ten, by which time I had been bullied into a pulp at school, so my father taught me how to box. I was too small, though, so I went to school with an old toffee hammer in my pocket and used it as a knuckle-duster on those who plagued me, calling me "Bubbles" and dumping me in the holly bushes.

My mother had always had a way, perhaps learned from her parents, of stating someone's name as if holding it up in calipers for inspection. She would say "Robert Louis Stevenson" with no preliminary, no other syllable, but offering R.L.S. in the round for wholesale evaluation, with no hint in her tone of how she would like anyone to respond. A conversation thus initiated would often go unpromisingly, at least to an outsider unattuned to the wealth of thought gathering in the name's penumbra.

"Robert Louis Stevenson," this time uttered like a conclusion she had been working toward for months. In such a context the very mention of one's own name had epic and threatening resonance; you never knew how to take it, once said, and you never quite knew how to say it either. Then she would say it a third time, heedless of implicit logic: "Robert Louis Stevenson," as if some interlocutor had accepted a challenge.

A long, creative silence would ensue.

Then the name again, as it summed up in intimate detail all the man's achievement, his every emotional vagary from babyhood to death, recalled with pleasure or incredulity. Stevenson she would name with some awe, but not, say, John Buchan or Eric Ambler. Words that followed, again loaded and pon-

derously evocative, would be "Imagine" and "Yes" and
"That's right." Little more was needed for an inaudible, unsung literary colloquy to happen, almost as if a class roll were
being called. The essence of our exchanges was in our whis-
pers, sighs, and nods:

"Bram Stoker!"

"Bram Stoker."

"Him."

"Imagine."

"Yes."

"Bram Stoker."

"Well."

A Pinter treadmill, this kind of talk implied an almost fa-
natical degree of family intimacy, but what it really meant was
disinclination to waste time talking. Evocative telegraphy I
came to call it in later years, admiring its curt dispatch and its
refusal to deal in time-honored bromides. Until I heard my
mother at it, I had never known how much *tone* could go into
one short utterance. You can imagine the choric awe that accompanied such a name as Beethoven or Bach, or even (in our
house) Charles Dickens or Alfred Lord Tennyson. Conceivably
we might have said such a word as *God* or *sin* and left it
resounding in midair while its connotations floated around
and at last settled like feathers on rusty wire, but we did not.
Few names got uttered, among them Richard Hillary the air
ace and Maunsel, one of the Derbyshire dales. She had said
America but without her telltale gusto; she let it lie, trying to
summon all her responses to it into one facial expression or a
singular, modulated sigh that still fell short of absolute exact-
ness. No one ever said *Africa*, of course, although my sister
and I sometimes whispered it to each other to see if Uncle
Douglas's twenty-three-year-old ghost would swoop down and
punish us. We dumbfoundedly marveled at his benighted

beauty, the shortness of his days, the vast number of things he was famous for. It was almost as if, at least as I felt it, the consummation of death had entered the clan long ago, disarming all other grief with his passing's suddenness and its hideous remoteness. Everyone, I thought, should have to die in Africa: pouf! and then a quick flurry of the shovel before anyone could even hold a golden mirror to the mouth just to make sure.

Looking at my mother, decade after decade, I sensed my vocal mind pronouncing her name as if she were a process hitherto unknown in biology. She was an enormous accretion of the best, the successful, the affectionately mild; her name had flash, zing, and melody, worthy to be murmured alongside Robert Louis Stevenson's. In her I sensed an obtuse longevity sending an antenna forward into the unknown region where muscle dried, mucus thickened, and the brain scrabbled frantically to match cause and effect. I wanted her always to be the brimful, terse mother she had been. She knew that names got onto gravestones. In some temple of abominable servitude, she had vowed to bury her children before giving in, just to keep things tidy, and to show she had not been irresponsible in having them.

Later, I became a paragon of muscle and accuracy, a mainstay of the cricket team, able to fling a ball at a batsman with fearsome speed and, by the same token, hit him in the face or the belly at will. Thus, in my first year of prowess, I evened old scores. I went into the holly bushes no more. Where had my strength come from? From *him,* my father said, nonetheless warning me not to hospitalize my former tormentors. From the *Noden* side, my mother said, recalling Uncle Douglas's genius when at bat; bowlers could never get him out, and he returned home exhausted after a long day's play, dark circles under his eyes, hardly able to speak, but victorious and aloof. Myself, I thought my power with the ball came from willpower and vision; I had seen what I wanted to do, and I did it. My father may have been right, though, for he too had been a fast bowler, and Uncle Douglas had been a batsman only, pure and perfect. My mother regretted her pet's evolution into a destroyer, though glad I had evolved an oblique way of defending myself. Pretty boys were lad-lasses, so called, in that school, and those few that existed there went on being bullied to the end of their days, having their privates exposed by the mob repeatedly to see if a sex change had happened overnight. It must have been excruciating for them. No wonder they joined forces with such a hearty as I'd become, hoping I would brutalize their torturers. And I did, thus garnering a waft of hero worship from boys with lisps and wavy flaxen hair. Where these boys came from, and why they were allowed to remain as they were, I had no idea. A lisp was one thing, but wavy hair and a tendency to tears were something else. I resented the notion that they assigned themselves to me, their altruistic warrior, not only for revenge and protection but also for training and toughening. I didn't want them on my plate, and I am afraid I ultimately left them in the lurch, witnessing their regular downfalls with what I did not know was *Schadenfreude* until, all on my own, I began toiling at German literature, starting with Ernst Jünger and Hermann Hesse, then the Penguin anthology of German poetry. My mother always saw the winsome, poetic side of me and cultivated it, becoming my aesthetic tutor and, eventually, my muse. Sufficient to know that, early on, I had a silky, pensive side wholly uncorrupted by my antics on the field of honor. One minute I'd be reading Tennyson, the next I'd be hurling the ball. I was a split personality, with friends on both sides of the split, as even now: I switch from Proust to heavyweight boxing with ease, knowing they have an elegance in common.

It was important to look tough, much as my mother grieved when I sloped off out, my hair hardened smooth with solidified brilliantine and glossed with water for a final armorlike sheen. It was important to scowl too and, within one's voice range, to bellow, or (my preference) to whistle tunelessly between one's teeth, suggesting a ruffian beneath the skin, slinking out at night with a toffee hammer to crack someone's skull. My mother saw me sliding down the chute to gangdom and ending up as a laborer or a miner; I did indeed join a gang, and sometimes led it, and we would capture other boys to give them The Snake, in which we twisted the skin of their arms simultaneously in two adjacent areas. Painful. Or we blind-folded them and pressed them with potato baked on a roaring fire. Having a sister, and a pretty one too, should civilize me, or so my mother thought, always pointing out what delicate ways my sister had. *She* was never plastered with mud or coal dust, bird droppings or dog do, from rolling about while wrestling. Alas, however, for my mother's pious or decent yearnings: my sister joined my gang and became a temporary outlaw, welcome because she had a small bicycle we could all ride when out on murderous missions in the Sitwell woods. All the same, my sister did not attract filth and became an object lesson in cleanliness when we went home. My mother inspected us closely and lamented her son, the ape and ragamuffin who obstinately refused to play piano. She saw the gulf widening between me and art; but who was she to know how arty I would become after my Tom Sawyer years?

I was most of all the object of her despair when, having been invited to parties of "nice" children, I was sent home for being rough. There were dances and presents at these fancy little gatherings, as there are in august universities even now. We played harmless games such as pinning the tail on the donkey and musical chairs. The trouble was that I often got into a scuffle with another rough boy and we knocked things over, teapots and cake stands, and sent potted meat sandwiches flying into the mellow, quiet fire in the grate. It must have been that I thought this society within society too exquisite and wanted a world closer to the adventure stories I read all the time. After my mother said, "If the lad wants to read, let him read," five closely printed periodicals aimed at boys came into the house on weekdays—on Monday *Adventure*, on Tuesday *The Wizard*, on Wednesday *The Skipper*, on Thursday *The Rover*, and on Friday *The Hotspur*. Sometimes on Saturday, for a treat, I got *The Champion* too. Some of these magazines were specialized (*The Hotspur* dealt with boys in high-priced schools and *The Rover*, as I best remember it, with anacondas, sharks, and octopuses). *The Champion*, to my mother's relief, proffered moral uplift, wanting boys to behave better, as if they had been to expensive private schools, as depicted in *The Boys' Own Paper*, a rigorously priggish upperclass organ I lusted after like a cinnamon smoker craving cocaine. Deep down, I wanted to better myself, but *The Boys' Own Paper* (*BOP* to the cognoscenti) was too costly. I eventually acquired it by giving up all but *Adventure*, *Rover*, and *The Hotspur*. My mother was right about bombarding me with print: she hit me with grammar, poetry, and Dickens; and the D. C. Thomson Company in Fetter Lane, London EC 3, provided me with pulp (where the *BOP* came from I have no idea, but maybe from the Crystal Palace or Rugby School itself). Canny tycoons had seen how lower-class boys enjoyed social climbing in what they read, spending brief sojourns among the fancy and the twee, the well-to-do and the stuckup. I too. I was an embryonic commando in poet's rags, or a poet in a yahoo bearskin. At some point, my mother recognized my artistic side and kept on plying it, lowering Tennyson and Wordsworth into the bear pit my body lived in.

On I moved, purging my violent side month after month, discerning how little future a rough boy had (it might even lose him his mother). I fell for aeronautics (to this day), little heeding those who told me my math was crratic, whereas I had some flair for languages. I loved French above all, as later on I did Latin and Greek. I was lumbering about, guided by a mother who had worked out a progress chart on which I graduated from rough to studious, from that to thoughtful or inventive—Bertrand Russell or Mitchell, designer not only of the Spitfire but of the Schneider Trophy seaplanes earlier on. Or Rilke or Blériot! She plied me with books about people who had done amazing things, and not just pianists and aviators. I began to wake up and wonder.

4

A Music Family

Romberg the Engineer

Light music, so called, was our familial cement, though as far as I can recall, my mother never played any. Sigmund Romberg, the Austro-Hungarian engineer turned operetta composer, was her favorite, and especially his hit of 1926, *The Desert Song*, from which one tune, "One Alone," held her in thrall. Sung in crisp, almost needling tones by Ann Ziegler and Webster Booth, "One Alone" became embossed in my brain, so much so that I forbear from quoting it now.

Ziegler and Booth were generating a sound of utmost purity backed by a moral stance cut in steel. So manicured their delivery was, so salivaless. Clearly they epitomized some standard of rectitude and austerity my mother missed in her relationship with my father, who put up with Romberg as best he could. So this, I used to think in my prepubertal muddle, is how people sing in the desert. This is a song of the sand, of caravansaries and sheikhs, Bedouins and Tuaregs. Obviously the male in question wore an army uniform complete with Sam Browne belt and revolver in its holster; his leather shone, his lanyard dried and tautened in the arid air. She, I languidly assumed, wore a frock, long and high-throated. They were saying there would never be anyone else for either of them. I liked their absolute way of putting it, and then I seemed to recall similar sentiments wailed by Nelson Eddy and Jeanette MacDonald, he in Mountie's getup, she in floral dress. In the background, what I presumed were the Rockies glistened with iceberg indifference. This was the domain of "Red Sails in the Sunset" (I always thought *Red* the subject of that sentence and *Sails* its verb, but I was wrong), Eric Coates's "Sleepy Lagoon," and the romantic violin of Albert Sandler from the Palm Court of some swankpot hotel. Grandiose romance stalked through our three-story home on Sunday afternoons, when the sticky dates came out and the nutcracker spat shrapnel hither and yon. It was the time for coziness, even in summer, and for the atmosphere of the house somehow to renew its tryst with bald-faced sentiment, full-blown romance, and, I suppose, the perpetual redawning of hope. Was it, I wonder, my mother's hope for a better life, or for the strength to endure the present one stoically? That she yearned was indisputable, but she was a closed emotional book in those days. The gramophone was scratchy, the records were soon worn out, the motor had to be rewound all the time, yet the overall mood was triumphant, even as my father insinuated his own tastes into the program, from Bach's "Air on the G String" and Handel's "Largo" to "Ave Maria" and Paul Robeson singing something—"Ayeeoko, ayeeoko"—from *Sanders of the River*. This last made my father happy, because some of his favorite reading was indeed Edgar Wallace's *Sanders of the River*, soon to be taboo in the house after Uncle Douglas's death. No more Africa.

Moved as I was by almost all music, at every age, I found little in Romberg to stir me, but I recognized the almost ritual peace it created in my mother, whose expression froze as the true witness curled its meticulous way into the fug of that tiny room. It was like a service, a holy promise. There were men out there, I guessed (the song implied it), of stunning fidelity, clean teeth, and flawless patriotism. It was a little bit of pseudo-Victorianism raised to the highest power: suasive and decent, mushy yet correct. Perhaps this was my first sample of politically correct love. At a lower level of romance, but to my mind a superior one of music, was something that came in on the radio (wireless we called it then) as the gramophone ground to a halt and the motor did its final wobble, hidden but alive. Carol Gibbons and his Savoy Hotel Orpheans played proto-jazz, mainly fox-trots to which guests were dancing in the lobby even as we listened. Snazzier music, this, with a different tempo, one of my favorite numbers being "Who Walks in When I Walk Out?", complementary opposite to "One Alone." Soon after, we actually owned a Ray Noble recording of this tune, but I have no idea who bought it or dropped it off. I treasured it for years, but it vanished in one of my mother's removals as her goods got mixed up and re-distributed. I suspect it broke, as 78s did, and made its way into the four winds on the garbage dump. What matters about Carol Gibbons and Ray Noble was that they brought me an aural glimpse of music that was going to obsess me for the rest of my days: not my mother's at all, though she tried to appreciate it as much as I came to relish hers, not her Romberg but her Beethoven and, later, her Bach. Also on the radio, often after our evening meal, I heard the BBC Jazz Club in-troduced by Harry Parry and Spike Hughes, biased in favor of jazz (blues and Dixieland) but occasionally offering something more streamlined, from the United States. I was spellbound by what I deduced was the true music of the U.S.A.—powerfully blasting brass, chortling saxes of sundry registers, drummers insane with drugs, crooners almost overcome by erotic or climactic excess. This sound was swing, to which I never wanted to dance; a tapping foot was enough, or a knife against a glass, a fork upon a plate. I adored the blatantly shaped riffs as they succeeded one another, vanished, and reappeared only slightly changed. Here was something melodic out of the industrial giant across the ocean. Here was a music that had come to stay, at least for me. No one else in the house fancied it, but I found in it the demonic, machine-age slickness I missed in jazz, which struck me as homemade, cumbersome, and careless. I was just a kid, and I was to know better. Yet that preference for swing has never left me, so I suppose I liked dance music after all, from the days when Fletcher Henderson was failing to make it with his orchestra to now, when imitations of the big bands of old tour the land and set feet a-tapping with the swing band favorites to which the fans first danced and then just listened, swaying their bodies in atavistic synch.

Gradually, as my collection of Brunswick and Parlophone records grew, my mother and I attempted serious talk about the blight that had invaded the house. Benny Goodman passed muster because, as I kept insisting, he also played clarinet with the Budapest String Quartet, though we seemed to have no recorded proof of that. So she went halfway toward such favorites of mine as "Why Don't You Do Right?" (composed when I was twelve), "Stompin' at the Savoy" (composed when I was six), and "King Porter Stomp" (composed when I was five). All of a sudden, she of the *arpeggiaturas* and *andante cantabiles* found me full of stomps, jumps, bounces, leaps, and rocks, though not too many rags. When Artie Shaw and his orchestra came out with a hepped-up, motoric version of a Romberg classic, "Softly as in a Morning Sunrise," she almost wept; the enemy had landed and was taking prisoners. She listened to them all patiently, with excruciated aversion, tartly dusting off the unexpended sarcasm of years. I expected something akin to what she said after my parents discovered that, instead of going to Sunday school, as required, I was hiding out in an old outdoor toilet. My paganism had begun to show. "If he doesn't want to go," my pagan father said, "he doesn't have to." One down, one to go. "If we make him go," my mother said, quoting from her Sermon on the Mount, "he'll end up becoming one of those liberals." I always wondered what she meant, but she would never say.

Taking the "A" Train

Into town on weekdays I would go to buy records or pick up little pamphlets issued by the Decca and Parlophone companies, telling who had just recorded what. These came free and tempted the spendthrift in me. They also appealed to my documentary side, explaining (if I was lucky) who the orchestra personnel had been on a certain recording date: Benny Goodman, Bunny Berigan, Nate Kazebier, Ralph Muzillo, Red Ballard, Jack Lacey, Toots Mondello, Hymie Schertzer, Arthur Rollini, Dick Clark, Frank Froeba, George van Eps, Harry Goodman, Gene Krupa. What standing you gained when you casually dropped such names as Kazebier, Muzillo, Mondello, Schertzer, and Froeba! Orchestras were always changing, but they mostly sounded like themselves, even when Jess Stacy replaced Frank Froeba at the piano, and Ziggy Elman replaced Pee Wee Irvin on the trumpet, and Harry James came in, or

Roy Eldridge, or Benny Carter, Teddy Wilson, Cootie Williams, Fletcher Henderson, or Nick Fatool. These, along with
the fighter aces of the Battle of Britain, were my heroes, many
of them unsung and not much recorded on any label. I told
my mother about them, in detail; she listened politely, then
shrugged. Who cared that Benny Goodman once played as
Shoeless John Jackson to preclude contractual problems? Here
I was, weighed down with esoterica from a domain she despised and knew I would outgrow. I, I wondered at a country
with such names as Schertzer, Froeba, van Eps, Krupa, and
Fatool! How exotic after a diet of my school buddies: Price,
Wilkinson, Ford, Bennett, Fisher. I wanted to go where the
wild names grew.

The magical, hyperrhythmic, organized thing called swing
was born on August 21, 1935—when I was five—at the Pal-
omar Ballroom in Los Angeles. But L.A. might just as well
have been on the moon; my mind had tuned in to something
remoter than the Hapsburg Empire, and it was no use, after
failing to beguile Mother with the music, working the anec-
dotal on her and telling how Eastern radio audiences had not
heard Goodman's orchestra on the *Let's Dance* programs because Xavier Cugat and Kel Murray came on first, and from
California, which of course heard all three. She looked puzzled
by such arcana and went about her business, peeling potatoes,
filling the cookie barrel, tending the coal fire in the grate. I
had become fascinated by what was distant and knew vaguely
that, one day, I would have to journey to the source of bliss,
to the country that spawned such magic. For the time being I
hit my books, but with an ever higher pile of 78s exquisitely
arranged in ascending order of merit. One week, Goodman

would be on top, with Basie underneath him, and Shaw beneath *him*, with the numbers too arranged according to merit.
Thus:

Goodman
Why Don't You Do Right?
And the Angels Sing
Sing, Sing, Sing
Avalon

Basie
Jumpin' at the Woodside
Swingin' the Blues
One O'clock Jump

Shaw
Copenhagen
Nightmare
Gloomy Sunday

Very neat, my mother said, but her praise warmed me little.
Instead, as I sorted through my favorites and sometimes had
to choose, say, Basie's version of a number over Goodman's,
a maze of overlapping hot tunes began to form in my head,
senseless yet unique, a prose of the also-rans: My heart stood
still I can't give you anything but love I'm yours out of nowhere prelude to a kiss let's dance undecided don't be that
way if I had you goodbye. The snazziest titles were Charlie
Barnet's, ranging from "Six Lessons from Madame La Zonga"
and "Pompton Turnpike" to "Murder at Peyton Hall" and
"Wild Mab of the Fish Pond." The most forced titles came
from Buddy Rich's Orchestra—"Backwoods Sideman," "Kil-

imanjaro Cookout," and "Waltz of the Mushroom Hunters."
Something almost literary surfaced in these phrases, akin to
the bizarre combinations of such poets as Cowley and Donne,
telling much about the country they came from, arresting my
brain with sharp, chromatic, risible images of a promised land.

But the literary aspect of this music pleased my mother not
at all; it was all too showy, too zany, for her, essentially for
the young, the raucous, the demented. I read to her the names
of those who wrote the tunes, often amounting to a mysterious
suffix. Who were, to list a few, Latouche-Fetter-Duke ("Taking a Chance on Love"), Marvell-Strachey-Link ("These Fool-
ish Things"), and Seitz-Lockhart ("The World Is Waiting for
the Sunrise")? So brief a mention did not, at least for me in
my early teens, translate into royalties. This was often the only
time the composers' names showed up. The numbers at once
linked themselves to a band or two, and that was that. My
mother rather enjoyed this recital of the unknown, admitting
that there were indeed serious composers the world had never
heard of—their works often appeared in examinations, con-
fronting the examinee out of the blue for an exercise in sight-
reading and impromptu playing. Her scholarly, antiquarian
side had responded, but without taking to the bumptious, outlandish music, in which, for a while, Duke Ellington came to
the fore with "Caravan," "Mood Indigo," and "Take the 'A'
Train." This music of his seemed so composed (deliberately
designed as well as poised), yet so providentially awkward, so
handmade; I missed in some of Ellington's numbers the big-
band whoosh I found in Basie, Shaw, and Goodman, as if a
whole fireworks factory were getting ready to blow up. The
numbers I enjoyed stayed with me forever, though, especially
"Take the 'A' Train," for which I made up at fourteen my
own lyrics, even though lyrics already existed. "You must take

that *A* Train," I murmured, "You *have* to take that *A* train /
Or else you'll never be in Harlem." I had no idea where Harlem was, but I eventually found out, though Pompton Turnpike, Peyton Hall, and the Lincoln took longer. My mother
appeared glad of the cultural plenty I was soaking up; it was
not just a musical craze but a genuine quest for exotic knowledge, as if I had suddenly taken to Lithuanian satire or Afghan
allegory. The Spitfire boy was not being buried in cacophony,
not quite, but he was busily comparing the faintness and diffidence of British bands—Geraldo, Mantovani, Ted Heath, the
Number One Balloon Squadron Dance Orchestra (By Permission of the Commanding Officer)—with the volcanic gusto of
the American ones, privately and obscurely registering the dif-
ference between a minor culture and a major one, one pinched
and inhibited, the other vital and barbaric. He knew what he
liked, and it would irrationally possess him long after he saw
at first hand the country that invented it. In the long run, for
literary reasons, he thought he ought to go to France, or even
Latin America, but he didn't; all the same, he felt ill at case in
the land he was born into, and even his mother detected a
wild, forth-faring passion in which, at first, music led him by
the nose toward more garish, savage landscapes, huge ethnic
dissonances, and a sense of unmediated, uproarious magic—
the country of the GI, who infested Europe, as Europeans said,
innocent and generous, loud and impolite. They responded
with india-rubber spontaneity to their swing, just as the British
crooned heartily along with their wartime linnets: Vera Lynn,
Ann Shelton, and others who primly and refinedly sang of
emotions that would outlive the war. I was a wartime kid with
a strong desire to be evacuated to America, where life writ
itself large and swing filled the streets. Has a would-be immigrant ever felt so aesthetic a pull?

But would the radio over there in America sing to me the song of the evacuee, as the BBC did?

> *Good night, children everywhere.*
> *Your mother thinks of you tonight,*
> *Lay your head upon your pillow,*
> *Don't be a babe or a weeping willow.*

Who composed this stern ditty I have no idea. Aimed at London children sent only so far from the metropolis as kept them safe and well within their parents' reach, it must have braced them no end as they got ready for bed or descended into the dank air raid shelter. Our part of the country was rated too dangerous for evacuees, so I presumed anyone sent to us (Poles, Dunkirk survivors) was being punished. No, I didn't want to hear the American version of the good night song, nor did I want my mother to croon it to me in my own home or under the cellar steps. You didn't desert your parents when the battle was at its height, not even to go to the land of swing. Later on, I heard a German slogan that comported well with the evacuee song: *Our walls are broken, but our hearts stand firm.* Sometimes, when Hitler and Goebbels addressed the benighted folk they governed, they chided them like British evacuees.

"Yes," my mother blurted in a fit of chastened anger, "it's a slogan for Londoners too. Blast those Germans. What on earth are we fighting about this time?"

"My stars!" she would exclaim when I turned up with a new album fresh from America but recorded, as the small print said, in a tiny studio during the Depression. Much of what excited me had been recorded in the mid-thirties, only some of it in the early forties. In Germany, my near-contemporaries had invented swing dancing while Hitler shinnied to power, but by 1939 swing dancing—not American, but the forerunner of jitterbug—was done for, and American records no longer made their way into Europe. I told my mother all this, hoping to sneak swing into her range of interests through the door of sociology; but the zany titles—"Clap Hands, Here Comes Charlie," for instance, a number originally written for Basie —set her exclaiming "My stars!" all over again. She meant that such a freak had never been predicted by her stars; it was not in her fate and should therefore be suspected of inferiority. Then came my Woody Herman phase, all on the Brunswick label, and she almost became interested, perhaps because Herman's music was so unlike music, some of it anyway, from "Things Ain't What They Used to Be" (an uncouth title, she thought) to "It Must Be Jelly 'Cause Jam Don't Shake Like That," which she found infectious and ribaldly silly, actually appreciating the lyrics ("Oh, Momma, you're so big and fat"). It was so far beyond her ken that she gave it the time of day, racking her brains for the reason. Were these drinking songs? No, I told her, but they *might* be; they were dancing songs, there to be chanted and stamped to. The record labels actually specified whether a number was a quickstep or a fox-trot (or whatever else). This appeased her somewhat; they were dances she knew, and even something as repetitious and banal as "Four or Five Times" exacted from her the smile of the penitent. How could she spurn something so daft and harmless? The lubricated frenzy of much swing upset her, but the moment the lunatics broke into simplistic song she forgave them the noise they'd been making and saw the whole affair as a crude form of literature. Even Tommy Dorsey and his orchestra's take of "Yes Indeed!" Did she, I wondered, somehow link the chanting of Woody Herman's band (or Herd) to the poetry of Tennyson? I once, in her later years, caught her watching a cow for some twenty minutes, perusing its quiddity, then explaining to me, since I'd asked, how many things it never thought about, how limited it was, yet how eminent a machine, and I suddenly saw that she was talking Plato: the cow had the virtue of performing an assigned function. In her late eighties she began to see things in the round; everything had its place because Creation, as we both called it, did incessant permutation of atoms, plunging entities of all shapes and sizes into incontestable being. She was not far, then, from Heidegger's notion of our being "thrown" into life. She saw the cow, and no doubt all the cattle her father had butchered, as sacred integers. Were we Buddhists? Even the wasp, the virus, the microbe, belonged. Perhaps you have to be almost ninety to sympathize with nature's incorrigible fidget, nudging creatures into being with not the merest interest in the usefulness of their collision, although creating in the fullness of experiment events propitious to life, helping it continue, or not. No doubt she never went as far as I had in imagining a first cause or deity; she was not the expressionist I grew up to be, so she never conceived of the first mover as a soul vast beyond proportion, now and then shoving a mutation into being, but only absentmindedly, his/her/its attention raw and primal, akin to Smeg of the Electra muttering, "I like them big tlabs." After all the eons, God came out with it, admitting that of all things, he fancied big ears. I could believe that, having long since subscribed to the involuntary automatism of nature. Just because savants racked their brains to understand nature, did that mean an even superior brain had created it? I thought not, but I kept this notion from my mother, who, all on her own, back then in the forties, *her* fifties, was trying to figure life out even as I assaulted her with primitive dance music accompanied by lyrics of the prohibitive underdog.

I come to this point and suddenly have no idea how to go on. "Treasured Memories of Mildred Noden West," it says on her gravestone, and I find it hard to get beyond that summary phrase arrived at by her children. Scalding memories re-create an absence I knew I would never be able to accept. Help me go on, I ask her beleaguered, overtaxed spirit, which sometimes comes through to me, warning me about method, murmuring, "That's the style" or "My stars, that's good." I reach this tearful halt because we, she and I in those midyears of World War II, were wondering what was worth committing our lives to. She had her answer: children, music, and literature. Literature was firmly third. Children and music were level-pegging. I, I was wasting my time on coarse music spattered with novelty phrasing; but, as I thought, I was "wasting" my time because so much of my mind I had assigned to the study of serious things—they were certainly creeping up on me at fifteen, darkening my mood, keeping me buried in a book. I have an undeveloped theory that children who grow up without TV develop early an unsolemn seriousness gleaned mainly from books, because things printed and bound seem permanent, trustworthy, talismanic. "Counterpoint," I told her. "The serious balances the other things? Isn't that all right? Is it, really?" She thought so, but she had not then done her inspection of the canonical cow, which would come forty years later. My memories of her appear through my memories of myself, and I keep reaching the moment at which I quietly desist and say I don't know her well enough even now. There was much she never said, and I had to extrapolate like mad even to get a hint of what wound her spring. How much better I would handle that period, and this recollection, if I had asked her the right questions. I was using my so-called music, and my literary leanings, to get to her, and she was immaculate, ensconced behind the barricade of Ludwig, Franz, Frédéric, Sergei, and Johann Sebastian, all staring me down as I leapt the fence, chanting, "It Must Be Jelly." Ridiculous? Behind this preliminary attempt fell the shadow of an appalling question to come: Did she equip me enough to withstand the time when she would not be there? I never thought so, but I was wrong. You work, she taught, to the greater glory of the unquenchable human spirit. I had heard this at school, implied in the endpapers of the Everyman Library books, but also stated in the sudden squalls of candid commentary from my teachers. The severe thing is that you have to do this for yourself, up by your bootstraps; she is not there patting my back, or cupping my forehead, denouncing raucous swing, and all I can do to vindicate myself is to report her aright, like Horatio, and apply the cautery. In a little cellophane envelope given away free at the post office, I keep among my stamps the photographs of her gravestone, which commemorates her love of music and cricket, the theory being that, each time I fumble for a stamp to send somewhere, I collide with photographs of the truth. And so, after a hundred years of correspondence, I might actually begin to accept things. Such the theory. I am, however, enough of a cheat to hold the see-through envelope in such a way that I see only the backs of the pictures while fishing out my stamp. How would she handle it? It was she who put the photograph of Uncle Douglas's grave on the mantelpiece in her bedroom: *memento mori* for over sixty years. She knew how harsh it is to "lose" someone, but had the guts to look loss in the eye.

To be born of heroic parents may be a blessing in the genes, but it is often hard to follow your parents' example, at least until you become old and the destroyer of delight begins to take you by the short hairs, turning you upside down and inside out. I mean the time in which you realize you are taking pills in order to go on taking pills. What my mother learned about herself while having her womb rotated from its wrong position, or my father about himself in his formative years at the machine gun, has no parallel in what I gleaned about me while pondering life in some university. During panic, I assumed, I would say almost anything. Time and again I quizzed them both about their brave bearing under onslaught, but learned little save the power of "thinking about something else." They had nothing to reveal about survival technique, almost as if, having come through an ordeal, they no longer had memory of it but had only an abstract of the complete situation. Courage allegorized, I gathered, whereas fear made things ever more vivid as long as you lived. Courage dealt in parables, fear in shocking close-ups. I was afraid of becoming sixteen or seventeen and thus losing the cozy privileges of the post-pubertal greenhorn, whose brash dance music his mother might hear out, whereas a couple of years later she would expect more of him and even question his taste in classical music, favoring instead the *Goldberg Variations* or *Le Tombeau de Couperin.*

Only once did my mother put up with Benny Goodman's "Sing, Sing, Sing," a ten-minute extravaganza full of solo drumming by Gene Krupa. In my responsive trance, or desperately in search of program music, I assumed the piece was about Sing Sing jail on a day of electrocution; hence the blasting, snarling trumpets (especially that of Ziggy Elman, all bottled-up kinesis) and the evocation of jungle talk. It was a musical portrait of a hideous place where hideous things were done, and never mind how much you tapped your foot (you were glad it wasn't strapped to the electric chair). "Raucous," she said. "Raushuss," my father added, resorting as ever to his own pronunciation. My mother hated most of all Krupa's drumming, denouncing it as unmusical and mindless, anticipating in her censure the words of Gunther Schuller in *The Swing Era*, in which he deplores Krupa's "monotonous drumming," "the horrors of 'Sing, Sing, Sing,' or the countless other examples of Krupa's rigidly relentless pounding (Jess Stacy was wont to call it 'Krupa's banging')." Myself, I enjoyed Krupa's bangabout, sealing in epitome the barbarism of the execution jail where Death Row was a banging of tin cups on bars and the lights dimmed when Old Sparky or whatever went on line. To this day, I get the same images from "Sing, Sing, Sing" as at thirteen or fifteen. My standards were documentary rather than musical, orgiastic rather than tasteful. Not even the Budapest String Quartet saved Benny from my mother's wrath for committing "Sing, Sing, Sing," which might just as well be a piece of exultant celebration celebrating the power of song. So much for alleged program music. The protonovelist in me insisted on finding in such pieces a train of specific events and a jugular plot—as in "Mission to Moscow," "When the Sun Comes Up," and "Caravan." Of course, as my mother readily conceded without liking anything I played, "Murder at Peyton Hall," "Pompton Turnpike," and "Between 18th and 19th on Chestnut Street" gave young pedants such as me a running start, although probably to nowhere. Rather like a spy, I was hunting images of America in its popular music (the swing of the swinging GIs who stole the hearts of the English girls and swept their brides off westward). It was not long, however, before I abandoned this tricky research, having discovered in the local lending library a run of novels by William Faulkner, the Chatto and Windus edition done in gold on blue. Images of America poured forth from the symphonic prose, easily more convincing than anything gleaned from short swing numbers. I still found the Count, the Duke, Benny, Woody, and Co. figures of stunning myth, somehow fusing them with Faulkner's prose. Whatever fusions I made, the effect was still musical, if muddled and rather farcical.

5

AVALON

The Holy Grail

Harmlessly I was being indoctrinated, mostly out of love.
Again and again my mother told me I could be anything I
wanted to be. I could even conquer math if I wanted it enough.
So I tried, conquering algebra (whose abstraction and semi-
verbal quality appealed to me) but flunking arithmetic altogether. Yet the tone and rhythm of my mother's urging made
constant inroads on my atavism. Between ten and fifteen, the
sea change took place, and I came out the other end a dedicated brainworker, deciding I would try for various university
scholarships in two years' time, not to please my mother, but
to consummate a strategy we both had dreamed up. I had to
work like mad, she said; I didn't know enough. She too had
slogged at theory and harmony, never mind actual playing. I
began to believe the harsh words that adorned my school re-

ports at term's end: "A boy of ability who does not work hard or concentrate"; "He has a good brain but wastes his time fighting." That sort of thing had stuck in me like an arrow when I was twelve, and I vowed to get my own back. Sent to the male teachers' staff room for advice on Cambridge scholarships, I was made to wait while the woodwork teacher thrashed me for whistling in class, and right in front of the more genial teacher whose advice I needed. They were lucky I didn't have a gun that day, or even a bow and arrow. On another occasion the headmaster thrashed me for giggling during school prayers. As I went out snarling, I met my mother, who had come to see him about some scholarship or other. It was a nifty piece of timing on his part; he had been gassed in World War I, and that was how he smelled. His son had tried to get into Oxford but had failed, which gave me some good prime-cut bittersweet later on that day.

"What do you expect?" my mother said. "They ended up in a third-rate school and will spend the rest of their days in it. You're shooting for the horizon, and they think you're too big for your boots." She who had braved the ogres of the Royal College of Music knew what she was talking about. I suddenly realized that the subjects I was good at were all taught by women who, when they peered at me, saw not a sow's ear but at least an imitation pearl worth driving hard for a year or two. My mother knew these women, who respected her RCM credentials, and the four of them developed an almost conspiratorial feeling. They would hone me until I was a torpedo, easy to launch, impossible to stop. They did not thrash.

At fifteen the long haul began, from French economics, advanced idioms, and the prose style of A. W. Kinglake's *Eothen*, to the imagery of *Macbeth*, Molière's use of the couplet, and the surreal in Maupassant's short stories. All of a sudden I couldn't get enough of literature, that hitherto distant orgy, and I had only a couple of years in which to prepare for the examiners, who, my dream team (mother plus three) told me, wanted to know what I did know, not what I didn't. Be brave and bold, they told me. Be different.

As should be obvious, when my mother introduced me to literature, she did something permanent, first of all getting me under my guard, getting literature to me before school gave me prejudices against it. After I had *had* to study *King Lear* and *Macbeth*, Wordsworth and Shelley, I had complaints having little to do with literature, drama, or poetry. The academic burden of interpreting a text, making sense of it, appealed to me no more when I was ten or twelve than it does now. Philosophy will clip an angel's wings, said Keats, and study-for-examination will dull the finest lines. So when my mother settled me down against her leg and read Tennyson to me, I was being brainwashed in a fashion most inspired. Not that she did not sometimes comment, mainly on the versification, explaining at one point how certain lines that did not rhyme had a rhyming manner, so much so that you thought you had heard a rhyme when none was there:

> *I thought I could not breathe in that fine air,*
> *That pure severity of perfect light.*
> *I yearned for warmth and colour, which I found*
> *In Lancelot!*

According to Mother, as I recall her commentary, the first line was one that breathed easily, the second reinforced the effect, though in less everyday language, the third restored us to casual expressiveness, and the fourth was a sudden release of intaken air. She said it more simply, insisting that I say the lines aloud, which was when I caught the point about pseu-

dorhyme. *Light* seemed to me to rhyme with *Lancelot,* which
was fitting. The rhythm was so emphatic that something akin
to rhyme carried you through; the clinching effect of rhythm
carried your ear through. As I look back on these lines, which
have stuck in my head ever since, I find them pale enough,
indeed making me yearn for warmth and color, but I can see
why she hoicked them out of context. No wonder she was
teaching English at Ruthin College, as well as music. She doted
on Tennyson, not so much for his full quiver of treachery and
falsehood, valor and perfection, ruin and misery, as for his
tapestry, though she was moved by the tale of Elaine, who
loved Lancelot and might have won him but for his chronic
infatuation with Guinevere. In the end, the fair Elaine, "the
lily maid of Astolat," fades and falls, her body floated down
the river to Camelot by a dumb old man. Having felt lilies, I
had some inkling of her skin. I soon developed a feeling for
the streamlined blank verse of Tennyson, recognizing in the
midst of my syncopated imagination (all that swing and jazz)
the ostensibly seamless quality of his writing; it was like a bolt
of material unrolled along a shiny counter that had a brass
rule attached to its one side.

> *O never harp nor horn,*
> *Nor aught we blow with breath, or touch with hand,*
> *Was like that music as it came; and then*
> *Stream'd through my cell a cold and silver beam,*
> *And down the long beam stole the Holy Grail.*

I twigged this at once because it brought to mind the long
shaft of light at the Electra, as down that long beam stole
(slunk, sloped) the holy grail of Godfrey Tearle and David
Niven, Googie Withers and Doris Day. Juvenile as I was, I had

a developed sense of light's nobility, its capacity to carry images that wrung the heart—something I suspect my mother
had always in mind when she went to the movies, more so
than when she went to church, although she had gone twice
there for the ritual known as "churching," when a mother
gave thanks for surviving the ordeal of childbirth. This was a
gynecological rite I never understood, as I indeed had come to
understand the ritual of the harvest festival, when new-cut
crops were draped across the altar: wheat, barley, rye. As I
got older I found I could fathom only the pagan side of organized religion; I had a strong Attis-Osiris streak in me,
strengthened by my immersion in poetry. By this token, then,
I might have seen "churching" in a pagan light too, with the
woman's organ peeled open wide for God's inspection, the
successful shiny ovaries laid bare for praise, and so on. I just
didn't know enough, though I had heard coarse village stories
of horny worthies who sneaked into church and laid their
dongs upon the altar to strengthen and thicken them. Surely
this was a more exciting technique than collecting sperm in a
chamber pot that sat under the bed until full, if ever.

From our *Idylls* studies I got the certain impression that
Queen Guinevere (Wenhaver to some) was never worth it. All
the pain and fuss she caused had every right to send her packing to a nunnery at Almesbury, where Arthur comes to see her
and forgive her. After a huge battle in the West, Arthur kills
Modred the traitor in single combat but is himself mortally
wounded. All this fighting stuff chimed in with my wartime
fixation and the map and flag studies my father and I did on
the kitchen table, pinning down advances and retreats and saying aloud the unpronounceable demolished towns. I got little
romance from the *Idylls*, but I suppose it wasn't bad to have
a two-thirds response: to the poetry and the mayhem, but not

the love element. I moaned, however, when my mother recited
without looking at her book the departure of Arthur's corpse,
which I discovered you could also call *corse:*

> *To the island-valley of Avilion;*
> *Where falls not hail, or rain, or any snow,*
> *Nor ever wind blows loudly; but it lies*
> *Deep-meadow'd, happy, fair with orchard lawns*
> *And bowery hollows crowned with summer sea.*

I liked "or any snow" for its intimation of a category beyond
categories; the author cared more about, against, snow than
about, against, hail or rain. Not the merest fraction of a snow-
flake fell: a perfect place for me. Later on, I looked at Tennyson's vocabulary and found it nebulous, vague, and
unobservant, I having by then read F. R. Leavis's *Revaluation.*
All the same, my mother had equipped me for close, sensuous
reading of imaginative writing. I was the only youth in my set
who regarded prose as something more than a minimal medium, a conveyor belt, for ideas. I always ended up seeing
more in a piece of writing than my fellows did, and I fancied
myself no end when, to make a point in specificity's and novelty's favor, I maltreated a piece of verse with unexpected
words. Thus

> *Merlin, who knew the range of all their arts,*
> *Had built the King his havens, ships, and halls,*
> *Was also bard and knew the starry heavens*

became

Merlin, who knew the range of all their radar,
Had built the Führer *his havens, ships, and 262s,*
Was also Gauleiter *and knew of starry Penemunde.*

A feeble enough attempt, it fleshed out my mother's teachings about words in context. The sustaining pedal on a piano had its counterpart in literature, she said; you held on to a word vocally in a self-aimed whisper. You never called it the "loud" pedal, or your mother hissed at you. Half a mile away, in Renishaw Hall off and on, another woman, Edith Sitwell, whom we had met, had written a book about Alexander Pope's poetry, and she too made the appeal for texture. It must have been in the air: *Alexander Pope*, one of Sitwell's favorite books, was published in 1930, the year of my birth.

Chimney Sweeps in the Rain

As well as to Tennyson, my mother led me to Wordsworth, the poet of daffodils and vernal woods, not a devotee of the long ago and far away but of the mysterious at-hand. What poet could appeal more to a child's vanity? To him, the child is unique, flawless, divine, inevitably corrupted in the long run, but for a few years a beautiful being who inspires everyone; and who needs inspiration better than an adult? She didn't stress this, but she certainly got through to me the child's marvelousness, and this is no doubt why I became a wanderer of the woodlands, the meadows, a collector of birds' eggs, a fisher for minnows and bullheads and sticklebacks, a gatherer of stones, bluebells, and glossy fallen feathers. In my own clumsy way I began to look at nature, wondering at its ceaseless abundance and why I felt so separate from it. I grew onions in jam jars, not as if I lived near Tintern Abbey, but to see what happened—in much the same spirit, uninspired by my mother,

as I took bits of strontium nitrate from my chemistry set and
sat them on the warm pipe in the bathroom, in which I then
slept. In the dark of bedtime they glowed with radiation, so
perhaps I was unwise to be messing with strontium at all. I
was groping for some holistic principle, not knowing then (*no
one* knew) that all things and creatures on this planet are made
of the same starstuff. Wordsworth had his own answer, of
course: pantheism, which envisioned a holy spirit informing
all things and at odds with reason:

> *One impulse from a vernal wood*
> *May teach you more of Man,*
> *Of moral evil and of good,*
> *Than all the sages can.*

Take heed of the daffodils, and you will pick up a gorgeous
emanation, a spirit surplus akin to the infinite fount of glory
and spirituality that attends birth. I did not altogether feel his
mysticism, by no means as heartily as I later did the musical
one of Vaughan Williams and Gerald Finzi, but I felt something which my mother and I, my father and sister, felt in
unison when out strolling almost at random in the Sitwell
woods. There was an uncoordinated splendor there that I
never quite figured out: why was it so soothing? The answer
must be that our response to things pastoral is atavistic; once
upon a time we had nothing else.

My mother also initiated me into something rare having to
do with Wordsworth: not so much his philosophy as his
method. Being a mystic, he faced a tough choice between watering his vision down too much, in which case it was not
special enough, and watering it down too little or not at all,
in which case it remained private, solipsistic. She did not use
the word *mystic,* but I got her drift: Wordsworth believed in

imagination, which confronted the mind with images not present to the senses—and excelled at it. I knew that much. So
how well did Wordsworth do? To my mind, to hers, splen-
didly, not least because he went at it all the time, making the
same sublime point in a hundred different ways. To my ear,
there was something almost drunken and impeded about the
famous lines

> *Not in entire forgetfulness,*
> *And not in utter nakedness,*
> *But trailing clouds of glory do we come*
> *From God, who is our home.*

Nowadays I call that a mantra, and back then my mother and
I said it aloud as exactly that. Wordsworth's woodland propaganda moved me more than the mumbo-jumbo of the Chris-
tian church. I was open to suasion, but it had to have some
touch of genius in it, and of joy too. Joy abounded in Wordsworth, and his "Ode on the Intimations of Immortality" and
"Lines Composed a Few Miles Above Tintern Abbey"
wormed their way into my being and linger still. I liked the
way the word *Immortality* softened the blow of its opposite,
mortality, which was what the poem was really about; "a Few
Miles Above" had for me the right ring of casual indeter-
minacy—he hadn't gone to *too* much trouble. I am obviously
stealing my mother's ideas here, the things she taught her
Ruthin pupils, but by fifteen I had worked up a little Wordsworth catechism that tested how he wrote against what he said
and helped me wonder aloud if something magical could be
effectively presented in general terms as distinct from stunning
images, say, that bounced you into "getting" him. I got something Wordsworthian from my walks, but did I get something
natural from Wordsworth?

Wordsworth's talk of the prison house growing around the young boy—shades of the prison house—was appropriate enough for successive stages of the Blitz. I lay in a rapture on the rug with my head against my mother's knee. We shared many a surreptitious grin as various scenes came back to us, shared then reshared. But there was always that weird smell of batteries put into the oven to warm or even to bake, so as to make them last longer. The reek of seared enamel was in the air all around us, like manured soot: smoke from the blazing city seven miles away, from the antiaircraft guns that pounded away all night; from the bombs that landed locally, even. Or it was from even farther away, from other holocausts, brought there by the prevailing wind. That I had smelled burning bodies I did not doubt; what a gross and unlikely context for the Hollywood idylls we watched, even for the war movies themselves. You sat in comfort, guaranteed two hours' entertainment, and that smell came after you—of locomotive yards, bus exhaust, of chimney sweeps in the rain. It was damp and cloying, not easily supplanted by cigarette or cigar smoke. It was the smell of my boyhood and early adolescence. I have always had an overkeen nose, whereas my mother did not. Was this not the smell that came off Hitler himself, the madman? Those condemned to be near him said he had a pong of smoke, no doubt proof of his link with the devil. At any rate, Hitler and his stench never went away; I bore him all the way to adulthood in both my mind's eye and my nose, and beyond. He was the foul fiend who had splintered my childhood. I did my best to enjoy the childhood vouchsafed me, perhaps by none other than William Wordsworth, but savage history blundered in and left it in tatters. On the other hand, the looks my mother and I exchanged implied how lucky we were, walking to yet another movie, walking back, finding out what would be shown next week. Somehow the movies kept us going in the immediate present while literature, Tennyson and Wordsworth anyway, took care of our metaphysical well-being, out on the perimeter, deep in the well where expert souls conjoined and comforted one another in the absence of angels.

One day, so as to make Spitfires, they said, workmen came and removed the iron railings that sat in front of our house. I knew you made Spitfires of aluminum, but I surmised the gates would become heavy guns or battleships. Suddenly we were naked, open to invasion, and it was years before workmen came back and installed a wooden fence, a wooden gate. Hosts of minor changes left us a little bit unnerved: air raid sirens, blackout felt against the windows, and nightly inspection by air raid wardens, who tapped on the door if you were showing a light. In time my mother became one of these wardens, An Official, so going to the cinema with her was like having a date with Churchill. In her face now and then, the worry showed. She had had two children only to lose them in some reckless bombardment, and down would topple both music and literature, etiquette and grammar. There was going to be no future. The Nazis would invade the island fortress, which was really an island on its beam ends, with only a scratch air force, an army armed with broomsticks, and not even a working knowledge of German. Had Hitler not funked invasion, he would have taken England in forty-eight hours. And here we were, savoring Doris Day, rehearsing subconsciously perhaps for domination by blonds.

Three Muses

Nearly everything I did was incongruous, even my efforts to build a secret weapon with my Erector set. As life, according to some antique rigmarole, became more serious, and I began to hear about the Wordsworth-like poems of Lamartine, as well as literature riper and perter, my three favorite teachers began to lean on me, demanding, challenging, urging, with never a mention of glistening rewards. I was to do my best because that was the thing to do. Excelling was an end in itself. This doctrine they shared with my mother. The means justified the means, whether or not it seemed Neronic. I do believe there was a theory behind such thinking, for which the Greeks had invented the word *entelechy:* a force urging you towards self-fulfillment, or (in Aristotle) self-fulfillment achieved. It was an appealing, though somewhat puritanical, idea, requiring much work and some sense of destiny.

Life, I learned, was not something to be lived impromptu from day to day, but schemed, like Hitler's onslaught on Russia. Where were this child's motors? Switch them on and see what he could do. So Gwendolyn Roberts, fierce and frail, in exquisite copperplate wrote out her own history of French literature in one sixty-page exercise book and *gave* it to me, telling me to learn it by heart. She then had me read yards of Victor Hugo and Alfred de Vigny, not forgetting Lamartine and his lake, then shouted me through Racine's *Phèdre*, Molière's *Le Bourgeois Gentilhomme*, and Rousseau's *Rêveries*, all in French.

"Yes," my mother said on one occasion, perhaps more than once (at this distance I recover the generic like an often-sung hymn rather than the particular), "I know she's a bit twitchy. But she's a distinguished woman who has proved herself. You can't afford to get on the wrong side of her. She doesn't think you're a sure thing by any means. To her, you're lazy and you fight too much. Why should anyone help such a time-waster? She can see right through you, my lad, just like some others I could mention. Take her on and she will give you a merry ride. Never mind how much she yells. It's a matter of how much she knows. You always liked French anyway. Don't be frightened of her. If you work hard for her, she will be as loyal to you as I am. She's Welsh, you know, and they have strong feelings." When Miss Roberts spoke, always vehemently, she blew faint spittle, her eyes filled with blood, and her small hands maneuvered right in front of your face. Intense, clamorous, punitive, she had a soul of mordant finesse; she knew what literature was for, all right, but she also knew what it was. It had ruined her life, it was all of life she had; it was her spouse, her holy of holies, her darkling plain. So much the better, then, if some young jackanapes happened along who showed even a scrap of interest in this canon; he could be shoved back into the fire and melted down, made into a new shape. I really felt in the hands of Merlin or Daedalus. If I stumbled, she would strangle me.

Surely my mother knew too much, not merely about me but about Miss Roberts, that lightweight *torera*. My mother was psychic; she understood Miss Roberts before even talking to her and emphasizing, as usual, the emotional impress of art, its irrational side: the palpitant wolf who seized her hands during the performance of a routine piece and made her play a whirlwind histrionic version. Miss Roberts, Mother informed me in her own way, may not have known much about the soul, but her mind was full of steam and precise matters accurately retained. Would I ever see, I asked my mother, a faint fleck of friendship or indulgence in those bulging bloodshot eyes? Not until I had pulled up some trees, I heard, and (I added) flung them far from me as redundant.

Frances Smith, my English teacher, who had studied at Birmingham University with the film-star-to-be Madeleine Carroll, where they both took Firsts (*Summas*) in English, was

just as stylish as Carroll, so much so that I always associated
Wordsworth and Co. with flashing nylons and incessantly
crossed and uncrossed legs. She believed in making you write
things out again and again until they were word perfect. Her
fiancé was killed in the war, but she never let on. The ring
stayed put, a talisman, and she chain-smoked with squinted
eyes; then she doubled her pancake makeup, creating for herself a burnished facial shield we often wondered at: almost a
batter.

Tiger? Tigress? I wondered, recognizing that my mother did
not respond to something flashy and swishy in this one, seeing
her as not puritanical enough. Frances Smith had made her
way in the world with svelte, spiky personality, and this my
mother deplored, disdaining to make comparisons with musical performers. Fanny Smith, as we called her, using the euphemism for rear end to indicate her neatly sheathed eroticism,
could eat little boys for breakfast and choke them with cigarette smoke. Miss Smith had class and style, and genuinely
adored panache in writing. She was keen in every way, and
sometimes woundedly sarcastic. *She* did not need to strangle
me; I would die of shame, having split an infinitive, say, or
committed an ambiguity that also had a passive construction
slap in the middle like a fir cone in a custard. Always, she told
me, try to reproduce the color and variety of the physical
world in what you write; don't be abstract; then you might be
able to make people concentrate on what you write rather than
on what they mindlessly live among. What a tyrant she was,
and how right. Fueled by this avenging angel, I was bound to
win a scholarship to heaven itself, and the whole idea had
begun with a whim on my part. Now I was riding a tiger, as
my mother said with entelechian glee.

Nonetheless, my mother knew that Fanny had had a kind
of Uncle Douglas, and she sympathized in the broadest way,

worrying a little about what she thought the movie-star aspect of this woman, but also knowing she could supply me with a lilt, a teasing, rhythmical quality. From Miss Smith, my mother decided, we needed no Wordsworth; we helped ourselves to him on our own, going far in our shared exploration of his most convoluted and simple-looking ideas. Fanny Smith made a specialty of Wordsworth, trespassing on my mother's terrain—who wished it had been Traherne, say, or Sir Walter Scott. But no, Fanny read aloud whole chunks from *The Prelude* with querulous flightiness, somehow incorporating into her voice a derisive element my mother found inappropriate; you read W.W. with almost clumsy devotion, being a country person in a rural context—no flash, no flair, but golden mumbling, at last recognizing what a bumpkin you were, contrasted with W.W.'s cosmos. And that was all right anyway, because God took care of you in a Wordsworth poem.

The third teacher in this trinity was Gene Knight, a woman of infinite, creative patience, who taught me Latin and less Greek, always commending Greek as more sinuous, more cursive. Perhaps so (I found Latin literature juicier, the Greek a bit thin and obvious, the less lavish of the two). After some preliminary sessions at school, and as the examination date neared, I would take the bus into town for coaching at her apartment, and it was there, over bread and butter, and tomato soup heated on a portable stove, that she introduced me to Proust, having me plow through the French and then rough-translate it orally. I had never read anything like it. This, she said, was vastly important work to know and to think about, especially Proust on love. All I remembered was Albertine on her bicycle. I labored, but it was many years later that I at last got the point and saw how inexhaustible *La Recherche* really was, not just for the French. I was then fifteen or sixteen, an unlikely prospect being brainwashed by a pioneer. Yet something stuck. Just having my canoe being lapped by the waters of that fastidious, holistic imagination gave me a push. I was thirty or so before I tuned in to Proust unencumbered and realized what I had been the unwitting custodian of for so long. Bach, however, whom my mother had always touted as *the* composer to grasp, took me much longer, until I realized that what I thought his twinkling amenity was more like completeness of sensibility rendered with aching grace. Gene Knight, in rough green tweed, had previously taught in a famous school in the city, but had left under a cloud. Their loss was my windfall; I could faintly detect in her life the steadiness, control, joy, and gratitude that literature had instilled in her. She longed to pass it on, whether to a scholarship candidate or to a whole class.

My mother responded to the yielding, gentle side of Miss Knight, discarding at once the notion, which toured the school, that she was more like a man than like a woman. It was clear, she said, Miss Knight did not see literature or art as a bag of Licorice Allsorts from which you tugged every now and then something to chew. Literature lived inside her, as music did in my mother, and so was not something to be whistled up like a dog or a sheep, but rather something that came to the definitive boil within, altering your life from minute to minute, all in secret. Don't copy what she says, Mother said, copy her habits—how she reads, how she compares, how she takes stock. How she says a particular word. Some of the words she said, I told my mother, happened to be Greek, or so Miss Knight said. So what? my mother answered. Say them aloud with her, and then you will have something worthwhile to say next time you want to say that word beginning with *b*. Chastened, I listened to Proust as if he were a Greek, which perhaps he was, and to Miss Knight's chanted lexicon as if it had come straight from *Remembrance of Words Past*. Suddenly there were licenses and liberties of all kinds open to me, such as I would never have had at the piano. I told my mother this, only to elicit a frown; it was clear that I did not understand music at all, but that literature might just keep me from going to waste through incessant thought of pawing a girl's knickers when the winds blew her gym slip high on the breezeway between classrooms.

These three somewhat derided spinsters, with whom I kept in touch, always addressed me, in person or by letter, as "West," as if I were a mustard or a port, retaining a formality of old, much as senior officers (officers senior to me) used my surname in the air force. I wondered what I would have done if my mother had addressed me in the same way, as if I were a walking mushroom. Those three dedicated, combustible Muses never became my friends, although my readers and critics. Utterly unlike one another, they each differently evoked my mother, though without my mother's almost superhuman dedication to art. What I received from them was a transcendental, proxy mothering in which their frustrated lives bloomed in the presence of masterworks.

It was as axiomatic as that. In the end, they all blinked at what they had produced, but never let slip a word of praise. There was no need. I had passed ages ago. Their altruistic duty was done, and that portion of their attenuated lives had been used up, given away, in the cause they had devoted themselves to. All they had received for their pains had been the vision of a boy in a hygienic bubble, pottering after them as he glimpsed the future. It was just possible, he realized, that literature was sufficient warrant for being on the planet at all. There was no need to look farther; this was how some people felt when they at last settled into the bosom of the marines, the church, or medicine. It had never occurred to me, although I had heard much propaganda about the life of science, technology, and business. Because I was a boy, with an announced passion for aeronautics, nobody had bothered to fill me in on the other life: of the arts. This was odd because, beyond the fifth form in our school, those who didn't go in for sciences were bundled together into an amorphous, catchall division known as Arts, even though to most that signified only teaching. Nobody that I knew was headed for philosophy, politics, writing, or even theology, yet all these came under the same umbrella. The study of literature was the preparation for all, much as the Oxford school of Classical Greats (*Literae Humaniores*— the more humane letters) became the launching pad for prime ministers, except, I reminded myself, clutching at scholiastic straws, for Eden (Persian) and Wilson (politics). These were the upper reaches of intellect and power. I delighted in the label that implied all the arts, but I shuddered at the narrowness of mind that dismissively lumped the nonsciences together as a rather pretentious mold.

Whatever I did in my own self-imposed scholarship examinations, into the sixth form (Arts) I would eventually go, there to become a ballerina or a parson, if I wished, but still attended by the three Muses. I could malinger there, if I found nothing better to do, until I was almost twenty, when the world would claim me. No one else seemed the least interested in sitting all the difficult papers I had put myself in for, so I presumed they knew where they were going and had comparable godparents looking after them. One girl, faultlessly distant from the likes of me, won a university medal for spoken French, and I thought: What chance have I? Anyone could speak it, my mother said, but who could *think* it? Just the reinforcement I needed: a major shove from headquarters. I vowed not to play the comparison game any longer. A man who aims at Mars does not resent those who ride a bicycle better than he on Earth. The way to speak French fluently was to rub Vaseline into your lips so they would stretch, and to have spare spittle behind your teeth to get the exact saliva blur that some French speakers cultivated. The world was full of secret ploys, best learned and practiced out of earshot.

There was not really a countdown, though I had some feelings I would later read about in what the astronauts wrote. In truth, I had read about these feelings in *The Rover* and *Adventure*. Ordinary life went on. My mother held back on her desire to have me learn to play the piano; she never mentioned it, seeing how much I had on my mind. I hit the books far too much, although never neglecting to prepare and learn by heart ostensibly majestic paragraphs I could slide into a more prosaic onset. I rehearsed the impromptu and adorned what I learned by heart, always wondering if it was all worth it. Just look at the Misses Roberts, Smith, and Knight, sacrificed on the cold altars of scansion, parsing, and précis (I did not know then that the altars had really been the *entente cordiale,* the Mighty Being, and *catharsis*). Not far away, in the gleaming bower of a fancy school we always defeated at cricket, lolled a carefree youth, groomed since he was seven, actually looking forward to the translation test from Hindustani, the essay on military imagery in Sidney's prose, the spoken Cantonese, the dreaded questions on economics and free trade in the general knowledge paper. He would breeze through all that and take my place, not even knowing my name. These nightmares I kept from my mother, but she saw my pallor and my twitch, how I kept blinking, and tried to cheer me up. I didn't have a cold, did I? I was like Stanley looking for Livingstone, and Stanley *had* found him, hadn't he? I would be one of the youngest candidates and allowed plenty of rope to hang myself with.

Suspecting I would never come back (drowned in the Cam or the Isis), I tried to piece my life together so as to leave behind me a coherent coat of arms. Or, if I came back gruesomely sea-changed, I wanted some memory of my better days, even if only to haunt me with fragments. I wanted to remember what I had been like, even if, by some miracle, I joined the select few and no longer belonged to anything save the college that had chosen me. Had my life so far been so bad? Apart from the bullying, had I done so poorly? I recapped, humming the song of myself, quizzed my father about model planes I'd built, my mother about the dishes I'd dried, how brave I had been at the dentist, and so on. True, I had hardly caught the eye of the girl who had won the gold medal for spoken French, but I did have the best collection of swing records in the village—nobody had as many Benny Goodmans or Woody Hermans as I, though Ken Honeybone led with Dorseys (Tommy and Jimmy) and Glenn Millers. Had I made my mark? As a budding cricketer, yes. I wondered why Geoff Magee, the cleverest boy in the school, was not trying for the scholarships. He was clever, he said (and ambidextrous too), because he never defecated; he could go for weeks without, and he truly stank of it, surrounded by a perpetual miasma of the byre, and, alas, imitated by his intellectual inferiors who, in order to excel, chose the way of constipation, bunging themselves up with arrowroot and with red rubber plugs filched from the chemistry lab.

6

MALADIES

Rimbaud's Drunken Boat

Even as a toddler I was aware of my mother's migraine bouts. In a darkened room she lay, severed from me, as unable to cook as to cuddle. I hated the disease even more when, at ten, I had my first attack, though without the nausea that afflicted my mother. My sister suffered in the same way. So there we were, with a half-blind father, singled out by the fates for familial punishment. As I grew older, migraine became the butt of some bitter levity, but it never went away. We suffered in the infancy of migraine theory, bandying around guesses about chocolate and old cheese, bright lights and nonstop worry. We had little idea what caused it, and the local doctors thought in terms of cold-water compresses and aspirin. The pain was acute, but the worst part of an attack was the illusion that some of the world was no longer there—the migraine

sufferer gets an incomplete, scintillating eyeful. From such dep-
rivation can come vertigo and dizziness, and an infernal sense
that you belong not to the human race but to some aberrant
cosmically branded species. If there had to be a philosophy
that coped with migraine, it would derive from Leibniz's solipsistic monads and Rimbaud's drunken boat. It amounted to
looking at the process of vision itself, though a process gone
badly askew. As I approached adolescence, I tried to see the
virtues of this blight even as I failed to complete an examination paper because I couldn't see it entire or got out at
cricket because I hadn't seen the ball as it sped toward me.
There was, surely, something privileged about it, giving an
extra cachet to all you did, making you feel more and more
different: singled out for special privilege.

My mother's view was percussive, as a pianist's would be.
She used about it words I rarely heard: "What the *hangment*
causes it I don't know, but I wish my children didn't have it."
Her mother had suffered from it too, and I saw an entire line
of twisted inheritance reaching back through the Victorian period to the Renaissance, joining those who mis-saw and
winced under the headache. I even wondered if many sensa-
tions credited as visionary had actually been migraine on the
prowl, and I supposed in my callous way that at least
thousands had bought the faith while under the headpress of
megrim, as it used to be called. The word means half-
headedness: you can see correctly with one side of your head
but not with the other, and vice versa. New culprits came and
went, from cocoa to coffee, but my mother suffered greatly
until someone invented Paramax, which can actually halt an
attack, whereas propranolol (which I take) precludes attacks
altogether. For some reason, propranolol does not suit meno-
pausal women.

Only the other day, my sister told me of an attack she had

had while driving on a throughway. She pulled over, took Paramax, and went and had a cup of tea. The attack waned, and she was able to drive home. It's worse if you are flying a plane or doing microsurgery. Migraine is no longer the scourge it used to be, but there are still some whom the drugs help little. I once calculated that my mother at sixty had lost almost seven years of her life to migraine. I would never lose the image of her supine, with a cold facecloth across her brow, her voice quavery, a white metal pail beside her to vomit into—and the shutters of the aspidistra room not only closed tight but sealed tight by the iron bar that came down and latched, as if to snub the nature of light itself. Much of her pain predated refrigeration, so she never had a chance at a face mask, cryogenic variety; I did but found it none too helpful. My father was uncannily sympathetic about the ailment he did not have, though he grew irate wondering why the Furies had fixed on his household with such punitive monotony. To be blinded by a shell was one thing, but to go half blind at random—dazzled, racked, nauseated—struck him as a low blow. Three, in fact. As time went on, he grew to like the universe less and less, while my mother saw migraine and other ills as a goad to further effort. She wanted the body to behave, and only will would succeed. In my bookish way I pondered the eagle that pecked at Prometheus's liver in the barren Caucasus, Philoctetes, who had a stinking wound, even Doctor Frankenstein's patchwork monster, and thought we are all deformed. Oh, for the deformed transformed. We are going to get worse and, in the end, will not be allowed to mix with healthy people. They will ship us to Molokai, the isle of lepers (as it then was). Migraine was the absurd flaw, not the tragic one, but it might get harsher and harsher, indeed producing tragic results, loading the odds against us until we gave up. Well, we rarely gave up, but we three walked in fear of bright lights, sunny days, chrome emblems on cars, the cuttle-fish-bone-white walls of squash courts, acres and acres of brilliant snow. It almost paid to go about with closed eyes, encased in sunglasses, and this I and my mother did, I eventually gaining a reputation for taking drugs (as the *Zeitgeist* construed me).

My mother had attacks all the way to ninety-four, although she quelled them if she had Paramax within reach. Inderal (or propranolol) keeps the beast at bay but makes you sleepy, which is okay for me, as I do not drive. To my mother, migraine was a gratuitous cross to bear, along with her defunct gallbladder and her ill-positioned womb. She more or less assumed that everyone had much the same, and took care to tell me of her friend who had had to have her toes amputated, another friend whose voice box had been removed, yet another who had been obliged to sacrifice a breast. As my mother came to see it, the human condition after thirty or forty was a ramshackle system of trade-offs, letting you go on living so long as you paid for the privilege with spent parts. Indeed, she saw it not as mere exchange, but as providential disintegration. To go on was to break down, to break down was to drop something off. Wasn't there, she once asked me, an old joke about a prisoner of war who "escaped" by having pieces of himself cut off and sent home, where bit by bit they carefully reassembled him, his heart the last to arrive? I had heard this, though my version existed to ridicule Germans, who failed to notice the prisoner was getting smaller. I told her about Rudolf Schwarzkogler, the artist of the razor blade, who sat in a store window and sliced bits off himself until, once again, there was almost nothing left. What remained of him was so paltry it could no longer slice anything off itself. For this, she gave me her old-fashioned steel-gray straight-eye look. Tell me another, she said. Now pull the other, my lad. But Schwarzkogler was real, and I later wrote a verbal portrait of him in *Portable People*. If, as I said elsewhere, illness is nature's art form (something almost as haphazard as evolution itself), then I might have found the idea in my mother's life rather than in her talk, she the stoic, I the expressionist. She couldn't see the point of having spanking-new babies, more or less intact, only to have them decay at increasing speed. Born only to breed, she thought, we spawn doomed replicas of ourselves, whose only purpose is to breed again without the faintest idea why. Sonata form made much more sense.

"My Little Music"

Throughout her life, my mother never got enough sleep, and I wonder if this brought about her many illnesses. How many hours we spent kneeling at, or leaning on, her bed of pain, stultifiedly praying or trying to tempt her back to health with magazines, gossip, pretty chiffon scarves, and aromatic cordials proffered with a shaking hand. Her lungs, her throat, her gallbladder, defied us, always giving her full value for their presence within her. It was no use arranging goblet-shaped tulips on the bedroom dressing table. Or bringing to her usually vigilant linguistic sense the snow and snot in daily discourse: " 'S no use," " 'S not *my* fault." A bleak curl of her lips greeted such voluntaries as these (mainly from me). When she was sick, she felt she'd let us down, and all her music pupils as well. She seemed vulnerable to almost every kind of infection, yet she had enormous powers of recovery. Fond of calling herself a creaking gate, she was rather a greased portcullis. Doctors came and went, most of them shaking their heads, but they were always wrong. Once, when I was in the air force, I got a wire to come home at once. I left in uniform and so startled her when I arrived—an almost unknown soldier bursting into the house—that she came out of her coma. I heard later that someone who had seen me in my peaked cap went around saying I'd got a job as a bus driver (it might have been the woman with the iron foot).

Her convalescences, always too short, were ovations of prudent delight, with the plainest of cookies served—oatmeal, arrowroot, digestive—and only the skimpiest of lean sandwiches, finger-sized and crumbly. She drank barley water and something akin to Gatorade. Her days of thick black stout and big slabs of ice cream were over, thanks to the gallbladder, and she force-fed herself a strange rubbery-tasting cream made from aluminum. I see her still, propped up at a bad angle, with the toggle-operated night-light shining wanly behind her over her shoulder, on her upper body a whole series of bed jackets, some from America. Even at her worst, or during a hurried convalescence, she never deigned to wear lipstick, though she sometimes applied a little rouge. She was as she was, she'd say; it was no use painting the lily just for a few visitors. It was during her recoveries that she began listening to a tiny radio, in the morning the news, during the rest of the day classical music. If she heard a piano, she turned up the volume. This radio she soon began to call "My Little Music," assigning it to one function only and, somehow, giving it credit for each composition that came along. It had a personality for her, this tiny box of electronics, soothing her for hours and signing off at just about the time she went to sleep. Her bed never looked slept in. She seemed not to have moved overnight. When she awoke feeling not so well, you knew because she left the radio mute.

And then, always, she got better, sometimes quite fast, and the parade of her friends began, clucking and giggling, protesting and exclaiming: "Ee," "Well, I never," "Just fancy," "What next?" and (as usual) "Well, I'll go to Trent," this signifying indignant astonishment; Trent was a nothing town in distant Nottinghamshire. In came the woman who added, "If you understand me, Mrs. West" to everything she said: "I know you're feeling a little better, if you understand me, Mrs. West. Some heal faster than others, if you understand me. . . ." I brought them cups of tea, shakily ascending the stairs, then lingering to see chatter initiated, spoons parked on saucers. No missions to be sent on, overhearing stuff from the stairs: He's growing, isn't he? Quite grown-up about it these days. It must be the good influence of a good home, all the healthy influences. I left them to their summations and got back to my upturned tea tray in one of the battleship-gray armchairs in the aspidistra room, next to the piano stool crammed with Bach and Beethoven and one chocolate box squashed into two dimensions from three, honored thus for some especial distinction of the contents long ago when the marzipan was fresh. Now I was right beneath my mother's bed and all the women examining her medicines, showing the little pots of pilchard paste they had brought her, the restorative pink buns, the bottles of fizzy drink, the little tubes of hand and lip balm, the delicate tissues made from cobwebs and candy floss. Trucks and buses rumbled by as I pushed my 2B pencil over the yellow tablet, wishing my mother would never be sick again. Whatever age I was, I fell into the same role, even after my father died in his sleep in the bed she always recovered in. I was the batman, the bull in the china shop, the local exhibit of what a surviving American looked like. It is uncanny to see her, as I do, not successively in three bedrooms—the three-story house; the bungalow or maisonette; the little flat a hundred miles away—but simultaneously, superimposed, so that the furniture clashes and the windows interfere with one another, and the doors bang. What remains the same, of course, is her trusting, relieved face, mustering a makeshift smile at whoever enters through one of the three doors. Yes, I thought, to be *roomed*: we are always being *enroomed*; we are never exposed on the wind-lashed heath with the lightning on our backs. There was never enough light in these rooms, even with all lamps blazing; it was bright enough for an invalid, but not good to write by.

Our standing joke, when I was home, was for her to say, "That boy hasn't written again," and for me to denounce him, adding that he was no doubt busy writing. "Well," she would say, "there'll probably be a letter tomorrow." She relished these agreeable pretenses when she had the world under control, and no mailman's whim was going to throw her. A bird in the hand was worth two in the afternoon delivery. She lived in a country whose first mail came at seven in the morning, the second at lunchtime. How astounding, I thought, to open your post with a marmalade-sticky knife. She did, and it was a beloved ritual, all the more when she had been ill and one of us crept up the stairs with half a dozen envelopes for her, next to her morning coffee. What pleasure that brought. Then she scanned the newspaper, scorning the nudes. As soon as the microbes and viruses relented, she loved her life with near-impetuous glee. She, the habitual recoverer, was beginning to feel invulnerable, never mind how sick she had been, once again proving the doctors wrong, certain she was made of the same teak as her mother, knowing the Almighty had recognized her business here was unfinished. She was popular. One husband came and offered to show her how much farther out of his body cavity his liver had pushed since she last saw it (or had the sight of it imposed on her). People brought their wounds for viewing, their quinsy for her to hear out, their latest tales of woe and indignation, as if, having been ill, she had been running the domain of capricious power and could exert an influence for good. Finally the humbled procession of her music students began again—akin to the one she led on the 30 bus to face the local examiners in Sheffield—at first not for music but to curtsey and mumble a few badly memorized formulas, to deliver minipackets of lavender or attar of roses and get as fast as possible out of there, where the air was tainted with burning tallow and doldrum sweat.

Pitched battles with the destroyer of delight: that was my version of my mother's illnesses; something reckless and obtuse saw her through, past the abyss of the Noden name, and renewed her for the fray. She had good genes. She needed them, having given birth to a daughter whose left hand bore an irregular crimson birthmark that bled, and a son who, when we were on holiday at the seaside, went and dated a waitress from our own hotel and soon after contracted pneumonia after playing soccer in the rain (in my delirium I cried out that I would smother the whole family in cloud). Instead of all that, and her many other trials, I would have liked to tempt her into a giddy laugh by reading aloud to her a letter from Spain, asking for my photo and my autograph:

Dear Friend Paul West:

First of all I give you congratulations due to your nice character, the marvellous you are as a writer, and as a person, I admire you a lot.

I want you to know that in Spain we love you so much and specially we, the young people. We love you and are for you a lot.

My name is Germa, I am twenty-one years old. I'm a Motel and my great dream is to become a great actress.

In order to finish this letter, I would like to ask you a favour. Would you mind sending me your signed photograph? I would like it very much.

Thanks a lot for everything and my great desire is
that you have all the luck of the world both in your
personal life as in your proffesional [sic] life.
I send you a kiss. With regards.

My mother, the stickler for correct English, would not have
smiled. "You were always taught," she'd have said, "that the
expression *a lot* is vulgar." She might have enjoyed the conceit
of a girl who was a motel and wanted to go one farther and
become an actress. My mother would have appreciated most
of all Germa Motel's signature, actually as big and epileptic
as that of Carlos Fuentes: six inches wide, two inches deep, all
whorls and curlicues. My eyes got giddy tracing it. "Swank,"
my mother would have said. "Pure disgusting swank."

Her father was a jovial, ruddy-faced, gullible man, a mason,
a churchwarden, part owner of the local soccer team, Eckington United, and of course a butcher. He was always giving
money or meat away: a soft touch, as Mother said, every
scrounger's philanthropist. In his last years he would get on
buses with no destination in mind or go down the street looking for people or shops long gone. He finally became incon-
tinent, and in the lodgings my mother had found for him, right
opposite his former shop, no one would change his clothes. So
my mother did this for him several times daily. There would
come a tap on the door, the signal: "Yes, he's gone again,
duck, there's no stopping him." Off went my mother to blot
him, with not a word. The decision to send him into a nursing
home seared her, but it was all she could do. Her two brothers
never visited their father, but my mother did. If only Douglas
had lived, her face said, we wouldn't be in this pickle. Grandfather Noden came back to our house to lie in state in the

front room, next to the aspidistra, only to be visited amid an aroma of damp and camphor by the local cleric, an arrogant, fat man who berated my mother for having sent her father away. His belt glided loosely over his paunch as he warmed to his theme, abusing my mother in sanctimonious jussives he had no doubt scribbled down beforehand. I told him to go and wished I had a chance to bowl at him, wounding him dead center in the dainty little frock that sits above the testicles, below the penis root.

7

A NEW MUSIC

Composers

Now begins the tale of how my mother's music proper began to take over my life, heaving in over the basis of swing without ever blotting it out. I became musically eclectic instead of obsessive, taking the bus to Sheffield to hear the Hallé Orchestra under John Barbirolli every Saturday night, and thus making the acquaintance of Ravel, Rachmaninoff, Elgar, Sibelius, and Mendelssohn. My first recording was Ravel's *Bolero* on three discs, the second Rachmaninoff's Second Piano Concerto, and I was soon into John Ireland, Delius, and Walton. Ironically, although I witnessed the conducting of Bernard Herrmann, an American, I never heard any of the American classical music that has delighted me since I finally encountered it in the sixties. Glad of a reprieve from swing, my mother actually settled down to listen with me, and we soon had an electrical record player. No more winding, and this machine plugged into the radio. I did not brood on the ease with which facilities improved as soon as I went classical, but I began to develop a slight guilt whenever I put on some swing. Besides, apart from some pretentious numbers (Artie Shaw's Concerto for Clarinet, for instance), swing records were ten inches in diameter whereas classical ones were twelve and had a ponderous, haloed look. *They* were serious. I was lonelier too: my record-collecting habits had carried over into classical, but those of my friends had not, and the friends I went to the Hallé concerts with did not buy records. To them, appreciation entailed going out somewhere to an assembly and being part of an audience. They would no more have thought of listening to music in private than they would have masturbated in public. I wondered why, for them, music had to be social, and seen to be so. The surreptitious, clandestine element I adored in moviegoing had its strongest counterpart in my private concerts; I considered moviegoing not a social act but a plunge into voluptuous darkness. As well, my concert-going buddies wore ties, whereas the only time I wore them was at school, where ties were required. After the concerts ended, we walked downhill to the Pond Street bus station, discussing the evening's program, and that was like the beginning of a parallel education—exactly what university life was going to be like, never mind where I ended up. I took the printed programs home and devoured them, even learned them by heart, and tried adapting some of their phrases to my literary studies, changing Elgar, say, to Kipling (which worked) or Ravel to Sully Prudhomme (which didn't). I found that some of the ways I felt about unparaphrasable music matched the way I felt about explicit literature, with a no-man's-land in between that attracted me no end and set me wondering about the ineffable versus the effable. How did one "eff" best?

These were the sounds of my head growing up. I had scores of questions about the serious music I heard, so I wore my mother out with them. She always knew the answer but worried about a son who now seemed to flounder between the three legs of his teenager's tripod: literature and the two musics, hers and that of Benny, the King of Swing. She made certain I understood that some works were exercises in musical notation, with no program behind them, whereas others were almost like movies. She spoke to me of tone poems. I spoke to her of Moussorgsky's *Pictures at an Exhibition* as one of the most specifically illustrative pieces I knew, and she responded with piano music: "The Rustle of Spring." Richard Addinsell's little pastiche, the *Warsaw Concerto*, written for the film *Dangerous Moonlight* (1941) after Rachmaninoff had turned the offer down, now swam into view, wholly unnoticed a few years earlier as I attended wholeheartedly to the plight of a concert pianist who joins a Royal Air Force bomber squadron: a man living in too many worlds—music, destruction, and Sally Gray. Perhaps Anton Walbrook was one of my wartime heroes, although not directly involved in the Battle of Britain. Now I saw him as the Polish pianist playing what sounded to me like derivative Rachmaninoff; but it was also the music of romantic sacrifice, of young men falling on fire from a great height, and I wasn't going to be picky. What was that little pseudoconcerto doing there? It was eking out the plot, to be sure, but it was also evincing the emotional hinterland of the military action. How many times the Electra offered that film I do not know, or how many times my mother and I sat through it *for the music* I do not know either; but we did, even after the war ended, in 1945. Rachmaninoff died in 1943.

Something else hindered my mother's musical career, even as an amateur pianist. Numbness of the hands began in her forties, the kind of numbness an Inderal-taker encounters on waking, to be followed by a tingling sensation before feeling comes back altogether. With my mother, the feeling did not come back, prompting her to seek various kinds of medical advice. In the end, she agreed to wear a neck brace for six, then twelve months, stalking about like a rebuffed swan. The theory was that the nerves in the back of her neck needed to be straightened; then those in her hands would come back to normal. For that year she kept her head commandingly erect (and afterward too), awaiting the day when her hands regained their proper use. It never came. True, her neck felt easier than before (she had never complained), but her hands were not hands for playing the piano with or, for that, sewing and knitting, which she loved to do. Many a time as her small radio played, I caught her looking at her fingers, motioning with them, playing an abstract midair prelude in time with the music, then looking up and slowing replacing her hands, like something she'd removed from its proper place.

We never knew the cause, if a single cause it was. Rheumatism, she said, and left it at that. Sometimes she would clap, almost punitively, and I without saying anything would think of "Clap Hands, Here Comes Charlie." She held her hands in a running stream from the hot-water tap and applied any number of so-called salves, rubbing hard at her knuckles and wrists, where she thought the trouble lurked. We all took turns massaging her fingers, though often converting the chore into an occasion for caresses, making her smile at the forgotten purpose. She held a hot-water bottle between them, arranged them in front of an electric heater equipped with artificial coals that glowed red. Those coals, she swore, had more feeling than her hands. It was no use. The condition did not become much worse, but it never improved, and when she tried to play the piano she never lasted long, no longer having the dexterity.

We kissed her hands, held them against us (our chests, under our arms), blew warm air onto them, but nothing helped. She would wear mittens indoors, but that only irritated her and made her feel hampered. Like Hans von Bülow, she could hear Chopin's body in his preludes, even, in a couple of measures, "the blood trickle (trills in the left hand)," but she began to refrain from such physical empathy with pianists of the past. In their work she felt their hands, and that was the last thing she wanted. She did go on listening, though, with an expression I found hard to define: she was more distant in the act, less agog, agreeably aloof from the mode of sound she adored. It was painful to see. Her neck collar had given her a new haughtiness of mien: nothing arrogant, but a resurrected fleck of her mother.

Everything runs down, I thought, vaguely remembering the second law of thermodynamics, but why does it have to be Mother? She was losing contact with music, whereas I had never made contact with the keyboard in the first place. I felt bad that I could not read a note of music, but my self-defense was that millions could already, so what was the use in that? My old, standard reason, already mentioned, insisted that she was *my* mother, and not the mother of all those who filed through the front door "to learn to play." I was being possessive; and besides, music wasn't our only link. I did feel humbled, though, at never having tried to have what she was losing. Yet the other side of that was this: I would never torment her by playing in her presence. These were the hands that kept my sister and me from butting forward, as if we were going to throw up, and they had to be revered. They were, and my sister and I each held a hand whenever we could, almost an echo of the way, when we walked the half-mile to the rail station to meet my father walking home, we would each take a hand and from either side shepherd our semi-blinded war hero home the rest of the way, effectively blocking the sidewalk.

Truth told, my mother had some sense of victory, having seen me veer toward classical music without any prompting from her, as if Ravel and Co. were some naturally superior tribe I had to join. It was self-evident. Yet I never backed away from swing and its syncopated riffs. It was all composing, the key word: you *composed* novels, poems, even paintings. "Write" seemed such a dim, helpless word, just as "writer" implied something nondescript; anyone who scribbled was a writer, whereas "composer" had about it something monumental and grave. If you were a composer, you put things together, with climactic finality. If this is a prejudice, I have never lost it, brainwashed as I was in my student days when I first happened upon Walter Pater's celebration of the work of art's gradually coming together from a thousand fragments, making a new whole never to be torn apart. And then, much later, there was Josef Suk's work About Mother, with the piano rambling and rejoicing around the beloved center.

The trouble with her hands was her *handi*cap, my mother said, scoring a verbal victory where no other was possible. I told her about the American composer Carl Ruggles, whom Henry Cowell had gone to see in Vermont. When Cowell arrived at the old schoolhouse Ruggles used as a studio, he found him at the piano, playing the same chordal cluster over and over again as if, says Virgil Thomson, "to pound the very life out of it." Asked what on earth he was doing, why he was torturing that single chord, Ruggles shouted back, "I'm giving it the test of time." She liked that, sensing the gesture included her. Some played with their elbows, I told her, or with the side of the hand, but the look she then gave me—of microscopic, tender skepticism, of good taste turned hostile—came to me all the way from Bach and Scarlatti, Chopin and Brahms. In vain did I talk to her of how Scarlatti had to be played with a flutter, with throwaway delicacy (which was why Horowitz, pounding and slamming, never got Scarlatti right); she knew that fisting or elbowing a piano was worse than crippling a pianist's hands. In vain I told her how Peggy Lee's exquisite version of "Why Don't You Do Right?" had come about only because she pestered Benny to make an arrangement of it for her; she had heard it sung by the blues singer Lil Green, and her own eventual version followed Green's every intonation in every detail, mimicking inflection and enunciation. Ovie Alston composed it, I told her. Or it was a guitarist called Joe McCoy. In 1936 the Harlem Hamfats recorded a number entitled "Weed Smoker's Dream (Why Don't You Do It Now?)." Gossip was one thing, she said, not treating a piano properly was another. She was not to be enticed by colorful irrelevance. She knew what was missing from her life and that there was going to be no remedy, as there had been for her brother George, suspended from the ceiling for hours. What, I said to her, if they had dangled *you* from the ceiling too, instead of sticking you in a surgical collar?

Couperin's Tomb

As a musical illiterate, I decided, I must woo my mother in nonmusical ways, which appealed to the nascent novelist in me. I boned up on the classical composers as I had on the swing instrumentalists and vocalists, gratifying my passion for anecdote and storing up quirks I could one day equip characters with. If I could not play for Mother, as my sister could, I might at least impress her on the level of data. She enjoyed a good story in that village of unselfconscious eccentrics, so she might appreciate bits of undercover truth. Ravel, I told her, never married, instead fixing his amorous attentions on his villa, "Belvedere" (to be pronounced Belvaydairy), which became his entire family. She thought the idea preposterous, but she could see a distant analogy between Ravel's living thus and the fate that befell old-age pensioners, living alone at last and nobody wanting to live with them.

"Was he quite alone, then?" She looked anxious about him.

"Just a maid and some Siamese cats."

"He was all right, then," she said.

He played with his cats, I told her, composed with them, wrote letters to his friends about them. She then made an observation about people's not being able to choose their companions in this life. They made do, she said.

Ravel spoke the language of cats, I explained. It was a language he had invented for them to understand, or it was theirs and he had picked it up. Who could know? The main thing about him was that he was abominably lonely, and people such as he feel obliged to cover up their loneliness, to give an impression of being exhausted by sheer sociability. The hermit feigns gregarious, I said, and she glanced at me sharply, put out by my attempt at pithiness.

Our chat about Ravel did not last much longer. *Bolero* pained both her and my father, though she could enjoy contemplating the piece's structure, whereas he, through clenched teeth, could clearly be seen damning Ravel and his cats, waking him up each time he had settled into a midevening nap. Ravel, I was telling her, fooled around a lot, meaning he played practical jokes, sometimes canting his head sideways while letting out a bird call, or (as he claimed) mimicking a seasick Chinaman by swathing an orange in a table napkin and then squeezing it mightily. You could hardly blame him for anything: in 1932, two years after I was born, he was in a car accident in Paris and eventually lost all power of coordination. He was in steady pain and had partial paralysis. In

the end, after the two and depression had worked their way
with him, he underwent an operation on his brain in 1937,
but never regained consciousness. One could only chill at the
obliteration of the mind that produced *Daphnis and Chloe*,
the Quartet in F, the two piano concertos, and, my personal
favorite, the *Introduction and Allegro*, which I called the Septet. I saw my mother evaluating and deciphering the long advance toward silence of so prodigious a musician. There it was
again, the inexorable wiping out someone of lustrous gifts, as
if a human were a sowbug on the sidewalk. She was moved,
but not beyond a slight cavil aimed at justice for Ravel.

She had remembered *The Tomb of Couperin*. Typical of her
to fix on Ravel's homage to a predecessor, the seventeenth-
century composer François Couperin-le-Grand, master of the
harpsichord. Then she added something personal, reminding
me that *The Tomb* also commemorated friends of his killed in
the Great War. Her face collapsed momentarily as she recited
for me some of the young men she knew among the war dead;
indeed, for a while it was a village without young men, apart
from my father and his shell-shocked cronies. Her face regained its tautness; once again she had assimilated the losses
of war, into her, through her, then flung them far behind her
as not her fault at all. She was all gratitude that my father and
her two elder brothers had come back from "the colors." Alfred, George, Thurman. Why should war be? Her perpetual
question aimed itself at the supreme being for not intervening
in human affairs. It was quite all right, meaning pertinent, to
tell her Ravel's Septet was written to show off the newly invented double-action harp, which could play all the notes of
the chromatic scale, but her mind was consumed just then with
cosmic inadequacies, and *Le Tombeau de Couperin*'s status as
an elegy was something she remembered as well as the music.
Had she ever played it? I sensed she had read it, perused it in

slow motion, or heard it played in London. I found and read aloud Roland-Manuel's tableau of Ravel's personality: "He had more frankness than elegance; more courtesy than cordiality; more sociability, more humor than abandon; more devotion to friendship than indulgence in camaraderie. And more ingenuousness than anything else." Thus his friend, biographer, and fellow composer. My mother paused after this casuistical catechism and then outdid Ravel himself for ingenuousness. "I think he was trying to say he was nice."

About Rachmaninoff we were brisker. He was having a nervous breakdown (at this her features stilled and set), but his grandmother nursed him back to health in Novgorod. When he returned to Moscow, he fell ill again, miserable and almost catatonic. So he went to see a physician named Dahl, who cured him through autosuggestion, fostering Rachmaninoff's now sapped confidence with repeated prophecies: "You will compose again. You will write a piano concerto. You will write with great ease." It worked. Rachmaninoff composed his second Piano Concerto and dedicated it to Dr. Dahl, with or without permission; maybe the issue never came up.

She thought this a beautiful story, could not remember if she had heard it before, thought she had, but with a different emphasis. Rachmaninoff's number 2, the second purchase in my record-buying career, was by no means as unpopular in the house as *Bolero*. Something homely and homemade appealed to my mother about this tale of a dedication, as had the elegiac side of *Le Tombeau*. As ever, she was dealing with things emotionally, in her so close to theory and harmony. Then we remembered this was the same man who had turned down the offer to compose the *Warsaw Concerto* for the film *Dangerous Moonlight*, and for a moment we could not link him to the music, or to the concept of the movie. It might have been so different. For three summers in a row, Rachmaninoff

had been living peacefully on Long Island Sound, but in 1942
he bought a small house in Beverly Hills (it sounded paradox-
ically unlikely) and said, "This is my last home on earth. Here
I will die." He began a final tour in 1943 but collapsed in
New Orleans and was brought back to California, where he
protested that music was being played quite close to him. Told
there was none, he said, "Then it is in my head." My mother
knew all about music in the head; it had to be, because she
grew up in an age of no recordings and so could never refresh
her aesthetic memory. With radio came reprieve and that epis-
temological mannerism of hers: whenever a phrase or fragment
crackled through, her face assumed a switched-on, automated
look; she was concentrating, bringing to bear in correct se-
quence the remainder of the work in almost joyous prediction.
She was a dab hand at that.

Mildredism

Surely a great deal has been lost when we can no longer
remember thus. When we can, a segment of the brain has actually become the work in question, has been given over to it,
so that remembering becomes not, as so often now, a process
of convenient synecdoche—a part standing for the whole or,
even worse, the whole (the title!) standing for all the parts—
but a loving enumeration. To remember, and so to ignore none
of the thousands of component parts, is akin perhaps to my
not entirely frivolous notion that instead of saying *Bleak
House*, intending all of that novel, we should pause, take a
breath, and then recite or read the novel in its entirety, fleshing
out to the nth the point we wish to make. I am joking, but I
do believe we need some way of discussing the arts that is
closer to the texture of the artifact. In universities especially,
the synecdoche principle reigns, every bit as much as it does

in book reviewing. Just a few novels stand for the American novel in the twentieth century: to know them, or roughly about them, is to know all. Just think how many books, some worthwhile, get published yearly but never get noticeably reviewed, mainly because of some quirk in the mind of a literary editor. I know one distinguished poet who has been reading Jean Genet's *The Miracle of the Rose* for some fifteen years, taking her time almost as if the pages of that novel had been pasted to the inside walls of her cell. Genet would have approved. And if that seems to fly in the face of what I have been saying about completeness (this person will never get through many books), I have to come down in favor of slow, minute perusal. Speed-readers beware. I once heard a journalist argue in favor of speed-reading Proust, which was a dumb thing to say because Proust himself, writing the long clauses and longer sentences he adores, makes you speed up anyway in order to keep abreast of what's going on. Dawdle, and you're sunk. Wherever we find style, we should honor it, and the best honor consists in eyeing it and savoring it as its gorgeous caravan passes by. If we don't, some of our best literature has gone to waste.

This doctrine is my mother's, of course. Let nothing, or as little as possible, go to waste. Heedless of titanic waste in the galaxies (supernovas and the like exploding), she set her mind on human genius and asked that it prevail, whether or not anyone attended to the resulting book, opera, canvas. Do the work incumbent on you, was her cry. You are not the public, nor are you the cognoscenti. Make your stuff and stand behind it. Like Melville, Havergal Brian, Van Gogh. Oh, she knew all right, and she made sure I knew too. So whenever I have thought, Oh, to hell with it, no one will ever take to this, her command has reared up in my brain, foreshortening the entire enterprise: do not try to write within the expectations of the reading public; give it your best shot, then leave it at that. She knew an author's ultimate fidelity is to the language, to each successive work, not to any school of appreciation, any band of admirers, not even the pedestrian ghost of the humdrum critic Clifton Fadiman. So there comes to be a ghost literature behind the accepted one, similar to the one the Soviets expunged from their encyclopedias: a literature of the untouted, one that slid unrecognized by, of enormous interest to cultural and aesthetic historians, of course, but relegated to the background and ultimately invisible because out of print. Civilization so called races onward with the merest cursory backward glance at the horn of plenty it has chosen to call its cultural heritage. Some years ago, at a talk in the Spanish Institute, New York City, I saluted the Lost Tribe of America and was gratified to find many reputable creative persons in the audience wanted to join that tribe. This is a nation whose novelists and poets feel overlooked, have nowhere near the standing and clout they do in France, whereas entertainers, poisonalities, hosts and compères and anchorpersons, rule the roost. Indeed, many helpless viewers assume these apparatuspeople are the true culture of the land, not the Aaron Coplands and the Charles Iveses, not the Faulkners and the Wallace Stevenses, not the Rauschenbergs and the Jackson Pollocks. In Ithaca once, where he had come to give a reading, the shortstory writer John Cheever told me he thought no worthwhile work ever went unpublished. I told him I never had that much faith in the good sense of publishers; but I couldn't think of a single example. That's the problem: it seals itself up, and a work has to have been published in order to be thought ignored. Only the published can be ignored. What idiocy, but no worse than what happens in Abram Tertz's (Andrei Sinyavski's) *The Trial Begins*: The public prosecutor and his victim are standing at a window, watching the crowd pass by.

The young man exclaims how wonderful it is, even though he has been accused, to watch the innocent passing by at their own speed, happy in their feckless delirium. No, the prosecutor tells him, *they* are the accused, and *you* the condemned. It was all one stage farther along. The unpublished, of potential merit, are doomed to be unpersons, whereas the published but ignored qualify for nonentity. To qualify for nonentity you have to have been somebody. So, some categories to be honored on days of uncommon compassion:

1. The unknown
2. The forgotten
3. The snubbed or overlooked
4. Those envied
5. Future pariahs

This is pure Mildredism, as I used to call my mother's most characteristic ways of looking at things. It requires the obstinate taking of an unpopular position and sticking to it even while being burned at the stake in bleakest Antarctica.

8

THE GROWTH
OF SERIOUSNESS

A Black Swath

Let me ponder for a moment the growth of seriousness. At school the girls thought I was *too* serious, as if I were already contemplating marriage, whereas, truth told, I had in mind some wanton depredations upon their private parts, savage removals of these girls to a quieter abode than school, say an old rusty lighthouse full of braziers, furnaces, clanking chains, and grinding pulleys. I was going to run my own Inquisition in there, hence the intent, businesslike look. Lon Chaney, Jr., Boris Karloff, and Bela Lugosi would give me a helping hand in creating my own chamber of horrors. I was that formidable offspring the *enfant noir*. Much of this horrid element came from the war, not least from several pictorial magazines having to do with the previous week's atrocities. In the aspidistra room, in the higher cupboard, sat a cardboard mailer in which

Covenants with Death, an anthology of war monstrosities, awaited its brave reader; in the back, half closed by a broken seal (I broke it), was a section of photographs not recommended for persons of sensitive disposition: mostly hangings and beheadings, eye gougings and eviscerated pregnant women. My eyes recoiled as my mind heaved. From this forbidden book, sent away for by my father the warrior, it was an easy step to the little league of *War Pictorial*, *War*, *War Illustrated*; weak on words, these magazines made you want to stay at home and never venture into Belgium, Poland, Finland. Blood was black. Sky was white. Skin was paper-frail. This was one way of losing your innocence, in a quite different way from sitting with Mother on a quiet, foggy afternoon over a pot of tea and mulling over my father's medals, proffered gently by her on a plinth of tissue paper, and finding out what each had been given for. My father always relived his own war; the new one, which began when I was nine, proved to him how popular war was, at least to the decision-makers. It was never that popular, he said, among sergeants; it all depended, however, on what else they could be doing—in civvy street, that was.

So the war, the bombing, the hotels entombing two hundred dead taken in their sleep, painted a black swath through my thinking. I just knew a childhood should not be like this. My mother, sister, and I, on the day war was declared, walked down Church Street, past Church Row, where my father was born, and down Gashouse Lane to the Old Mill, there to buy bags of apples in case of food shortages. We came away laden, but sure of the future. To some children, the war was a wheeze, almost to be enjoyed, until the bombs came too near and a land mine cruising toward us on its parachute removed an entire field. In other ways, there was just too much bad news for any child to sustain a carefree pose. Sooner or later the misery caught up with us, and the grievous influxes—of Polish refugees possessed of only what they stood up in, of English or French troops from the Dunkirk retreat, trembling and waiting to be fed. Those from hell were always hungry, poor at sleeping, and almost afraid to talk. Right there in the street there was much demonstration of bayoneting: how to shove the body off the blade with your boot. I think the inevitable darkness of life reached me in scenes such as these, though I buried it behind brain fodder more wholesome.

After fifteen, as I became better at thinking, I began to develop a sense of humor: not much, perhaps, but at least life's absurdity rendered into wordplay, which does not always endear itself. Death, I thought, so vast and unknown, makes even the tiniest joys magnificent through the obscene disproportion of it to them. The pun, I found, abolished time and category, cause and effect, creating holistic pandemonium. One of my favorites came from Clive of India, who, after capturing the province of Sind, sent home a wire that read *"Peccavi"*—I have sinned. I rejoiced in this for weeks, although nobody else seemed to like it. No wonder I made a boy called Clive the hero of my only straightforward autobiographical novel. It was a thank-you. I am trying here to distinguish not between high and low seriousness but between serious and trivial. My downfall, I am sure, was that I had a pale face, which attracted various village commentators, asking my mother what was wrong with her lad. I myself called these newtheads the palePaulers, akin to those who thought my name too sissy and went out of their way to call me Peter instead. I was besieged by people whose ironclad preconceptions would save me from liberalism or effeminacy. Pallor, though, coupled with seriousnessness made you a lurking menace, as likely to side with the Nazis as to give your life for the *colors*. You would almost certainly inflict a wasting disease on anyone you touched, and you surely had a hollow backbone from all the sperm you had spilled. *Pale* to me, though, connoted intellectual, high-minded, and foreign. I aspired to some of these qualities. My mother was pale, my father ruddy. She and I composed good reasons for being pale: our blood went straight from our necks to our brains, bypassing our faces. Ruddy was agrarian (my father snorted), pale was urban. We were full of specious reasons, happiest when the lights went down at the Electra and everyone was pale. Pallor, I learned, came from being cooped up indoors, hitting the books, writing examinations, and eventually you began to look rather waxy, as if you needed a good scraping. Does it matter, Mommy? I asked her time and again, and then we looked at all the faces in the encyclopedia and the dictionary: all were pale; the rosy-cheeked ones had not made it through the sieve of history. And they never would. I tried not to grow up thinking myself accursed; you could be serious without necessarily being pale; but, if you were both, it wouldn't kill you. She and I, I decided, were on the philosophical side, as likely to wonder why there had to be theories of music in the first place, or acts in a play, as to bury our noses in a nest of new-blown peonies just for effect. So we were monkish, anemic creatures of the night, with mushrooming ideas.

I told my father about Ravel and Co., but all he did was shrug and mutter, "Bloody Frogs." Dead or alive, they were all the same to him, treacherous or loyal. Perhaps there is an ineradicable gulf between palefaces and redskins, or between Brahmins and rednecks; it is certainly not to be bridged during discussions of warfare. I had discovered myself one of the main grievers of war; my mother bore the continual imprint of an African elegy; we were surrounded by a deadly element amid which nobody moved or spoke, nobody burped or stiffened the upper lip; a domain of rotting acquiescences without tennis, chocolate cake, or maternal kisses, and we hated it because we did not feel appropriate to it: the wrong kind of cannon fodder. Those willing to go through life pale as ghosts should never have to die. Or so we reasoned.

"Like Banquo," my mother said.

"Him," I answered, trying to quote.

"Ah," my mother said, "but he was bloody, not in the rude sense. Blood-*boltered?*"

She knew the play better than I, who had been obliged to read it for dissection three or four times. The bloody play was covered in blood from the scholars' and critics' lances. My mind went far afield, plucked out of the going like the airplane that veers sideways and ahead from a squadron going over, so as to create the missing-man formation, when a pilot has bought the farm. There is something crudely moving in that sudden subtraction, that suction away of the lost aviator's living counterpart. Nothing but air in his place, making you shudder and a tight, infernal hand grasp your rectum, warning you that your turn will be soon. It was the same when my father went out to drink a pint with his fellow survivors of the Great War. They would order a half-pint for an anonymous absent friend, as they called him, and would explain on leaving—unselfconscious about having said it hundreds of times before—that this gentleman felt a bit off-color tonight, so perhaps the landlord would quaff it in his memory. My mother hardly ever went drinking with my father, so I, who eventually went now and then, told her about his rituals, and she said yes, that was what the war had done to him, that was what wars did to you unless. . . . She never finished.

These borrowed shudders, these intuitings of fatality and the miserable paraphernalia that uselessly accompanied it, told me

I wasn't so much a serious child as a morbid one. I was soft, which is what the word means, both hypersensitive and neurotic, and I was getting by through various subterfuges, from symbolism to cricket. I was the lamb in the ravening beast's bulletproof vest, I was the avenging demon in the white face the palePaulers deplored. My mother could see that, like one of those appalling Nazi rockets, V-1 and V-2, I was aimed skyward, destined to get away and, if I returned, to come back from some other place I thought of as home. It took a long time to do it, and memories of my native village have fueled and enticed me ever since. I was born amid a swarm of engaging characters who had not the least idea of the figure they cut on the human stage. Of such characters literature gets born, and the sense that once upon a time you were somewhere.

My neurasthenia (old-fashioned word sounding graver than neurosis) had often to do with minor matters such as perhaps having to wear glasses. I had long discussions of this with Gerald Roberts, a boy on the brink of eye failure, and we considered the many facets of something artificial affixed to you or, as with my pacemaker many years later, inside you. Our conclusion was that appearances were arbitrary and malleable; it was just possible that glasses would *improve* someone's looks, blurring the beauty that lay beneath only to make it more evident. Something like that ran through our tender minds: a huge topic, really, having to do with the homogeneous and the way it cheats categories. I was concerned because my mother had been obliged to wear "specs" for reading, and it troubled me to see her transformed into a semi-robot, although in the end her spectacles altered her everyday appearance less than the neck collar, which gave her a military guardsman's stance, a "stiff brace."

Something was cooking in my impressionable head. When

I went to Saturday afternoon matinees and saw the latest episode of *The Thunder Riders*, I marveled at the "ugly" helmets
worn by each Thunder Rider; underneath, they were rather
handsome men, like Gene Autry and Tom Mix. I was sick-
eningly interested in disguises and fronts, knowing I wore one
myself, and in their success or failure. Gas masks, bandits'
faces concealed by neckerchief triangles, gruesome masks
manufactured for Guy Fawkes Night, the lard-thick grease-
paint worn by itinerant actors who came to my school and
put on performances of *King Lear* and *Macbeth*, the goggles
and oxygen masks that pilots wore: all these occupied my
mind more than they need have done, except I was overpowered by the way words concealed the world, abridged and two-
dimensionalized it. To talk, to write, to read, was not really
to be among the world of things but to be lost, as Plato would
say, among appearances, approximations—unless the words
bonded together had uncommon specificity. I knew which demon tempted me, and I needed to know his limits. To go into
words was just possibly to fall into the abyss of heedlessness.

Only much later, after I was fifty, did I come to a full re-
alization of what words had done for me. I sit facing the small
clearing on my desk I keep free of the all-devouring mess of
books, papers, and journals, and I tell myself it is the same
size as the space between fork and knife on my mother's dining
table. Here I perch, like a submarine commander or an astro-
naut, attending to nothing outside the area of the typewriter.
That is the arena where I have to get things right, never mind
what unseemly clutter surrounds me. This, in the dead of
night, after all other minds have shut down and cars are no
longer backfiring, is the catbird seat, where I clip and paste
little slips over errors, big slips over bungled sentences several
lines long, and sometimes retype whole pages that have gone

astray from the first. I feel like some ancient stonemason, a monk illuminating a letter, and remind myself this is a savage, noble calling, capable of driving you insane if you don't watch your perfectionism. *My* keyboard, as my mother always said it was, part resentfully, observing how tiny it was compared to that on a piano. Then we would get off into the most futile of dialogues about words versus notes, and a permutation of "meaningful" signs as distinct from one of abstract ones. We were different, though; I always construed this debate of ours, done with palpable sweetness and some jollity, as a religious one. She always had Bach to fall back on, and his mood of reverential acquiescence amassed in tiers of well-tempered gentleness. She outgrew Beethoven, as did I. I would always come to Bach, she said; his was a healthier approach in a world as cruel and inexplicable as this. Beethoven only got you worked up and deluded you that you could do something assertive about it. Parallel to Beethoven, I had found André Malraux with his doctrines of "virile fraternity" and his desire to carve a scar on the universe: melodramatic and grandiose (you can do it by stealing Indochinese statuary, as he did). T. E. Lawrence belonged in there somewhere too, another go-getter who ended up gotten. I knew my mother was right (when was she not about art and moral dilemmas?), but I didn't know enough to agree with her. Clipping my little rectangles of paper exactly to size, gluing the backs, then adjusting them into position on the page with tweezers and an implement otherwise used for ingrowing toenails, I felt like a brain surgeon, negotiating flaps and tags, touching areas nobody had touched before, making the case under my hands come out well. For this, you need steady hands, and those I have. Such is part of the homemade magic that attends my nightly devotions, for three or four hours, rather like my mother at her sewing machine or her keyboard, with the windows barred and the gas fire blazing into points of flame above the slotted white pottery cages it made glow red.

When I was with her, "over there" on an annual visit, watching her health wax and wane, I would go slightly crazy to think that New York then (ten at night, say) was just coming to life, and California was only just finishing lunch. I sat there as at a vigil, and that is what I keep now. This cramped position with room only for the machine is in part my penance, let us say a penance born of nostalgia. I could clear my desk after a labor of some fifty hours (it has taken the mess years to build up) and operate under entirely different auspices, but I would lose that hemmed-in hunch I associate with the space between knife and fork, the upturned tea tray wedged between the arms of a gray armchair. My hindrances keep memory fresh as I hear Bach on the boom box, as almost always during this book, wondering at the weird sense he gives of space-flight metallurgy: you soar with him to a humbling destination, and he lets you down so gradually into it. As long as Bach plays, Mother smiles, but she will stand for no Schnittke, Scriabin, Shostakovich, Rubbra, Copland, Villa-Lobos, Britten, and countless others. I don't mind. How little I know of the world. I go to Washington, D.C., and discover my room-service waiter is an authority on Bulgarian composers, telling me to listen to the works of Pancho Vladiperov; he scrawls it for me on a piece of the *Washington Post*. I haven't done so yet, but I will. Long after the work was first performed, I heard Gerald Finzi's setting of Wordsworth poems, including those my mother and I said by heart together. By then I was a fan of his music, though of his orchestral work mainly, and I liked this particular work for its long orchestral preamble. A bit irked when the countertenor voice started up, I leaned on Wordsworth recollected in my mother's voice rather than in my own. Or was it the voice of us both, saying the words in unison, a little ragged and uncertain, but appreciative and personable, she motioning to me with the same slight beckon of her face I had seen her address to music pupils, I with a sideways cant of my neck acknowledging her. Competing with the countertenor, we had to work from memory because the printed text was missing (slid into the album, it had slid out at some point, never to reappear; perhaps it ended up in the United States by accident, as so many things did, bundled into my suitcase at the last minute, attached to some file or folder by catastrophic surface tension). By the same token, I left things behind, often a book, that would then start on its journey from Derbyshire, where my mother lived until she was ninety, to Empingham in Rutlandshire, where my sister lived. There was a continual shuffle of stuff on both sides of the Atlantic.

My mother and I spent many hours peering at the TV screen together, most often tennis (she harangued the players by their first names—Virginia, Chris, Yvonne) and cricket (she harangued these players too, but by their surnames, a stern headmaster rebuking naughty boys). These were blissful, inordinate occasions, requiring only the scantest conversation and little wedges of fresh pork pie to sustain us during play. The times I remember best, however, had nothing to do with TV. The BBC broadcast a cricket match in its entirety, so we would sit outside in the broiling sun with a small occasional table between us, each in a deck chair, and submit to the spell of the commentators, well trained as they were to conjure up the scene at the game. There we sat, hour after hour, with the radio she called her Little Music playing at about medium volume, transfixed by voices and sounds from another planet, even while we sipped tea from outside china, nibbled pilchard-paste sandwiches and a biscuit or two. We perspired and tanned, prisoners of delectable mind's eye, captured by verbal evocations of the greensward and the watching crowd. On some of these grounds I had myself actually played the same game when I was fitter, and I got an elegiac feeling from our cricket afternoons, yet overpowered by other feelings of near-unanimity, reunion, the prospect of many more afternoons to come, doing the same thing. The miracle and mystery of it all consisted in what was missing. We had to reach toward the game in our minds, cued by the ever-so-precise and casually poetic commentators: usually one Australian, two Brits, plus a West Indian or an Indian or a Pakistani. When an especially dramatic play came about, my mother would lift her finger as if conducting or hearkening, and I would just about stop breathing. Some paramount enchantment was afoot, requiring undue concentration, and she wanted it not to go to waste. Lounging there, looking at the less than charming roofs of other homes, we would lure ourselves further into the potential spell, hearing incredulously that someone had hit the ball so far and so high it had left the ground altogether, bounced once on top of a passing bus, and crashed into the top window of a bed-and-breakfast opposite. What happened then was that they used another ball, of roughly the same wear and tear, without waiting for the lost one to be found, which it quite often was not. The extraordinary moment ended, yet not without reminding me how often my mother had dunked a spoon into a pot of hot tea and then raised it slightly higher than the pot. This was her signal for conversation to halt. She did the same with anything at hand: a napkin ring, a spectacle case, a hair clip, commanding instant good-natured obedience. Often she accompanied this gesture with a kind of imperious shrug, as if galvanized, thus accentuating the surcease in her bodily movements. And, especially at table, as being there intensified attention, we would all four give a little twitch (or a shrug) and freeze until she signaled the end of the trance by lowering her spoon, or whatever. Such were the antics of our family when things were passing through. We left the meaning vague, but the ritual was crisp, and I recall it most and most movingly from the years when my mother and I, an infatuated couple, lay in the sun construing the commentary on the game we loved. One small finger sandwich of fish paste on white bread restores the habit to me at once, pitted by only a few exclamations ("Ee," "Heavens," "Just imagine"). We thought we would last forever thus, that the matches would never end, the radio never run down. When the tea grew cool, we made some fresh, and when the sandwiches gave out we went inside and found the next batch, under cellophane. Alas, outdoor listening perished when color TV swept us away into its dominant never-never land; we chafed to see the players' faces, boots, the action of the bat, the scurry of the ball. You could always close your eyes, though, and spend a few critical minutes noting how unvisual was the commentary that knew you were watching. My mother never lost her quaint, teasing way of giving a sudden start and freezing, which I would always echo with a sudden body movement, knowing that something was going over: a moment of inestimably enigmatic aura. Hold your breath. Still your fingers. Do not blink. You were allowed one flinch before you froze, and mine was to raise my eyebrows. Sometimes, later in the hiatus she had caused, my mother would exclaim "Sithee," "Bill," "Ships," or something more explanatory: I think there's somebody out there, peeping in.

Was this, I used to wonder, when Ludwig van Beethoven, patrolling pianos in the provinces, moved in by moonlight? Or was it Uncle Douglas, our broken Prometheus, come to check his butterflies? Or my mother, quite prankish at times, was just having her way with us, exerting a delicate inclusive power over her beloved ones, drilling them or rehearsing them for ethereal roles in another world. I never quite knew what was going on, but the magic of her tricks invades me still, and I think she had found a bizarre way of expressing ineffable joy as her dearest people and things amassed at the table (all) or outside on the lawn (she and I). Trying to get her joy into words, she had never quite managed it, being too moved by occasion; but she knew she had to make us aware of how pleased she was, so she settled for a gesture that seemed stern but was one of the faint curlicues of spiritual ravishment. Imagine, she was saying: *we have all this*. It mattered little that all this wasn't very much, materially speaking; what mattered was ecstasy, like seriousness, weaving its plenteous way in and out of time in the presence of the marmalade, the fish paste, the tannic soothing tea.

I had to relate the majesty of her salient moments to her incessant nightly coughing; I could not do it, but I knew she would never cough again if I got her to Arizona (where I myself discovered how to breathe at last), but I was unlikely to get her there. She had misgivings about being too far from the toilet when aboard the jet, and none of my reassurances made any headway with her. It would have been the same plotting to go to her eidolon of Greece (Athens would have put paid to her anyway, whereas Carefree would not). Rheumatism, glaucoma, gallbladder, numbness, migraines, split skin on her hands, all convinced her of her membership in something doomed. The Almighty was just too lazy to come and get us. *I* would have said that mortality was nickeling and diming us to death, but she didn't speak in that fashion. She knew an extra ailment could always be tagged on to an already creaking vehicle. Looking at us three with his one eye, my father, who had seen hell close-up for three years, was not the man to panic, and he never did, watching the evolution of his wife and children with the distant fervor of a mystic. Whatever happened would happen; he never wanted anything to improve, or anything to change. He knew all about Wordsworth's wise passivity, whereas my mother was a Victorian, passionate about progress, and an existentialist of the agnostic school. The part of her that connived with Bach was the miraculous element in her. Nowadays I would call it chromatic surrender: waving all flags while drowning, or creating a sublime variation on a theme with the last blurt of energy you had. It did not puzzle her in the least that Ravel's dead friends entombed with Couperin became the occasion for some dainty music. Why, she had wondered, should a human try to be so perfect when the Almighty, who plies us with wonders, has so feckless and vengeful a hand? The absurdity of life freed her for aestheticism, cricket, and poetry, all of them gratuitous voluntaries independent of heartbreak. Throughout her life, she isolated heartbreak like a murrain and let it be.

Pregnant Pauses

Coming back to her sudden suspensions of daily activity, I recognize that I have ignored something. During those short spells of hovering or stall, what she brought us up against was the is-ness of things, the quiet flurry of mere existence. You sensed your peristalsis, your heart doing what it would always try to do, your eye wetting itself. Instead of being committed to some hectic and no doubt laudable activity, we were auscultating the basis of life itself, without demand or prejudice. What to call it, this benign habit of hers? The fancy version is inertia in the interstices, but I recoil from that to something humbler, at least in the saying: the hush halt. This was when you attended, if of a mind to do so, to the space between the end of tock and the start of tick, or between a sentence's pe-

riod and the uppercase letter of the next sentence. This was
when the unproctored intervals of life came into their own and
haunted you with the image of what you were like against the
background of flow and seepage, pulse and minute degenera-
tion. This was when you had no big enterprise in mind, not
even the munching of a pear afloat in sweetened syrup (as we
ate things in those days, improved by the can). It was this view
of life that frightened people when they lay in intensive care
or spent the night on the floor at an airport. Obliged to pit
their basic self against a huge design of vital processes, most
people look away, for something more arresting, more appetizing, to linger on. When the mind fixes on a lubricant for
ten minutes, it becomes uneasy, being fed data patently un-
worthy of its attention. At the same time it matures, turns
incontinently vivid, knowing it has at last trafficked with the
ineradicable font of life.

Such was the effect, on me at least, of my mother's nearly
saying "Perpend," the verb of Polonius the wiseacre, who
means the same thing as she. My mother was a pause-maker,
delighted to stem the flow of human enterprise. It was as if
she blew a whistle. Ever since, I have blown one for myself,
almost eager to get into situations that would bore everyone
else to death—usually, *waiting,* for which I have no gift, but
I do have a philosophical desire. Consider what underwrites
us, I think; amass the fluids and sludges we have in common.
Esteem the lymph in the blood, the wax in the ear. These are
not going to be the subjects of radiant odes, but they might
be inexhaustible objects of contemplation for the next fifty of
our years. Enough had gone wrong with my mother's body
for her to have an acute sense of its softness as a machine
without ever having seen, say, movies of surgery in which,
observed by an intrusive little camera, the intestines glisten and
slither, look-alikes in the main but gifted with devastatingly

exact functions. This interior image may not be anyone's turn-on, not when compared with the superb expressiveness of a human face, but we did not invent any of it, though we keep on getting better at tampering with it. I think my mother was a quiddity-savorer, when peering at a cow or halting the give-and-take at a meal. As when hearing piano music she saw the staves and notes behind it, anterior to it, so did she discern behind bright and beautiful behavior at the dinner table our blueprints in motion, not intercepted from a whisper on the wind, but maybe in a gurgle, a hiccup, an oceanic sound in the ear, a surge in the thighs as a nerve settled down for the night. And of course in the mind, at last attending to its very own manger, fidgeted into being—liver, kidney, heart, blad-der, pancreas—by an evolution that barely knew where it was headed and developed through something like opportunistic improvisation. So, then, the hush halt, devised by my mother —no, it was never that deliberate—*fallen into* by her in the teeth of sociability, as if what mattered most about life was what folk wiped away, dabbed at, left on Band-Aids, or shrank from viewing at all. A greasy view maybe, appropriate for a butcher's daughter (her father's calling no doubt helped her to look life in the eye, look at it in the raw). Only the other day I saw, in some newsreel footage, my first human spleen, badly mangled but even so looking like something you might acquire at a tripe shop in the English Midlands, along with other offal, for a good fry-up with onions. So far, of course, we have not had a poet of the pancreas, a bard of the bladder, but that day will come. If Marin Marais, at the beginning of the eighteenth century, could compose a piece for viola da gamba mimicking successive steps of an operation for stone in the bladder, then there is surely hope for us. This is program music with a ven-geance, its pointers in French citing the operating table, the patient's trembling at the sight of it, the incision and the re-

moval of the stone, the almost complete loss of breath, the
flow of blood, and then the putting back to bed of the patient.
There follow, in rejoicing, three jolly dances entitled *Les Re-
levailles*, which accompany the churching of a woman after
childbirth. We witness the birth of a stone and the churching,
then, of a man. Here is the actual music (Marin Marais is the
distinguished virtuoso in the movie *All the Mornings of the
World*):

In our not altogether honorable quest for the poetic in subjects hitherto deemed barbaric, we have not gone far enough
into the alien region, conquering telephone poles and aircraft
as we have but still unable to smelt the toilet, the blast furnace,
the telephone, into something lyrical. Their day will come, perhaps in poetry composed aboard a spaceship or at least a mission to Mars. Marin Marais was doing rather well for a man
of his time, but only because he possessed what S. T. Coleridge
called the esemplastic power, which welded all into one. All
things are ripe for poetry, Rilke said, heedless of the aesthetic
bureaucracy that proclaims otherwise. A few prosaic poems
about baseball are not enough to vindicate imagination at the

very end of the twentieth century. Music has advanced faster than literature: there are pieces of music based on ionization, pulsars, and solar radiation, some of them evocative and daring. My mother was a holist without ever needing or using the word, and those pregnant pauses of hers, as when Proust's heart misses a beat, were vacuums for the world of phenomena to fill in. She dammed up the flow of stuff and parted the Red Sea. Nature flowed in all over again. She was like a drill instructor, deeply reverent of Creation while wondering why it ever had to be created. I drank this from her cup, suspicious ever afterward of "works" that stopped the world too long so as to make a statement about it: *The Prelude, The Mill on the Floss, The Forsyte Saga.* Works that left you with more than was there before—*Remembrance of Things Past, Finnegans Wake, Moby-Dick*—were a different matter, needing to be read and reread lifelong, mulled over like certain salient actions in one's life.

As for music, serious music, toward which I was moving like a land yacht in a sandstorm, I began wondering if Gerald Finzi had been wise to incorporate Wordsworth's words into his tone poem; he should rather have rendered his total impression wordlessly, *in his own art,* as Scriabin might have done. To hear Wordsworth's words elongated and twisted gives a weird impression of the Procrustean composer at work. Always I made lists, the first of them including *Bolero* and Rachmaninoff's Second Piano Concerto, but I soon ditched them for braver works, such as Shostakovitch's Fifth and Brahms's Second Symphony. I have made hundreds of lists and thrown them away, secretly fulfilling my mother as I noted an item heard on the radio, then transferred it to the master list with which, a couple of times a year, I march into Tower Records (often cannoning into the Plexiglas door beyond the see-through revolving one) and go alphabetically in pursuit of what I have to have. Usually I find half of what I'm looking for and order the rest. I could order them all and never move, but the idea of an expedition devoted solely to music (no interfering notion of literature) emboldens my amateur heart and keeps me loyal. It has been so since I discovered American composers, perhaps beginning with Roy Harris's superb Third Symphony, seamless and fluent, once picked out as one of the finest symphonies in the repertoire: full of demonstrative confidence verging on bravura and a smack of inevitability to its swiftly delivered transformations. Perhaps his is the outer radiance that comes from interior anger. He writes as naturally as paper absorbing moisture from air.

9

‖ Rooms in College ‖

The French

Dazzle them, said my mentors at school on the eve of my departure to sit the scholarship examinations, almost in the mood of Diaghilev's "*Étonne moi!*" addressed to Jean Cocteau, who was surely capable of just that. Time and again Cocteau shook Diaghilev. Too much of my knowledge was based on rumor, as I found out later, but I did know Rousseau's "The Reveries of a Solitary Walker" almost by heart and saw that one of his notions—that of at least being *different*—I must not only take to heart but, during my candidate week, enact with choreographic zeal. It was like being obliged, within the confines of those much-climbed-over ancient college walls, to soar beyond the human race, yet without going too high. If one achieved excessive solar apogee, he would seem better suited to a rest clinic in the provinces than to a court near the Cam or an Isis quad; or, at worst, a teacher-training college where half-wits hard-earned massive parchments to mount on their walls. The main thing, however, was to fly.

"Yes, dazzle them," my mother said, "but give them a good helping of facts too. If you know any. It's no use giving them well-whipped froth. Use the dates of things. Quote what you're talking about. Write things out before you write them into your answer. Try and remember as many details as you can, as if you'd *been* there."

"Where?" I asked her, knowing I was going to flunk.

"Any century you like," she breezily answered. "Or at a certain place in a piece of music." I knew what she meant, but my wayward policeman's mind was more inclined to have noticed the thin, humble rings worn by bank tellers as they shuffled fortunes to and fro over the mahogany.

At a lower level of befuddlement, well below the suicidal masochism of seeming too brilliant to live, there was the near-felony of perhaps winning a scholarship for committing crimes which, in a more prosaic ordeal, would get you failed. With nothing to lose and all to gain, I felt like a gambler, more Dostoevskian than Vegas-ian, not even sure that what I was planking down on the light or the dark blue was valid currency at all, but giddily conscious of tempting the fates without getting into debt. The whole test was a lottery, even the winner uncertain of being allocated to the college of his preference, since many colleges examined jointly and then competed among themselves, over the port and walnuts, for the cream.

A solider student than I would have worried about being unable to march his data past the reviewing stand, whereas I, exhorted to twist the questions to my needs, had a field day throughout that initial baptism-of-fire week, sidestepping and weaving, importing irrelevance like ersatz gold leaf, discarding the examination papers themselves, boldly setting and answering (or begging!) questions of my own. My strategy, I now see, was to drive the examiners out of their minds into mine. Look! my scribbled voluntaries cried, *I am here. This is what I do. Choose me*, not them (or me among the few). After thirty-five writing hours, two interviews, and a return train journey from Cambridge with my swollen suitcase in the tourniquet of my bathrobe's cord, I began the wait. An award would bring a telegram, followed a week later by a one-line listing, precious as lutetium, of my name among others in the better-class newspapers. In the event, I received a letter, in which the master of the college explained that I could not even be admitted as a "commoner," which was Oxbridgese (a hangover from days of bone-deep grace and favor) for entrance unfunded. I had not even been allowed in.

Too tired to think in terms of catastrophe, I leniently heard out my elders, who said it had all been practice; I had not been expected to "pull up any trees," except by some eleventh-hour egregious act of God. Next year I would go again, trying for both universities, but only in English: no more French, which upset me (I preferred its literature to ours, and still do). Back to my books I went, a chastened performing animal, sacrificing Rousseau to Wordsworth, Rabelais to Swift, my innermost mind haunted by that heady sample of the promised land, Sidney Sussex College, where Oliver Cromwell had been. I yearned dismally for the flyblown quiet of its coal-smoky rooms (even a candidate had "rooms" and not just a room), the atmospheric seethe of the fire in the grate, the kettle that boiled thereon like a hydraulic ally, the rind-stiff marmalade on the dead toast in the dining hall, the tamed lawns in the courts, the continual bells, the river-sweet fog. It had all gone up in some kind of smoke, or down, like a severed head, into the enormous picnic basket into which one laid one's script when one's best had been done, or the proctor said stop.

"Don't *fret* about it," my mother told me. "Don't *stew*. There's always another chance next year."

She was right, but I didn't want to wait a year. Having all of a sudden formed a taste for the Oxbridge life, I wanted to clinch things then and there.

"Perhaps it was the French," I said.

"Well," my mother said, "just listen to your father on the French, and the Belgians too. You might have been better off with German."

"Oh," I answered, in some such words as these (taking care not to stir her up too much, or we would see bags of sugar hitting the walls and have to dig out the flashlights to go and find her later on): "You mean something tidy and orderly, like the Germans in the stuff I read. I think I'll bank it all on English, a language I seem to know."

"You know some of it," she teased. "Nobody knows all of it; it's huge."

"Certainly not the Germans or the French or the Belgians," I said. I imagined a language like an iceberg, most of it out of sight and earshot, never used by its speakers. What could you do with such a monster? As much as possible, even if it took another fifty years. My mother and I were being examined together, almost as if in music, she the sorceress, I the prosing toad.

Tully

One could, I discovered, form a crush on a place, on a college's official polychrome scarf, its plumbing, its amber evening lamps. That I had been born for (though not into) all this

I had no doubt, and that I had, like the gauche prince of leg-
end, been shut out I could not believe. A god had failed, and
also a boy. Imagine my puerile agonizings as, in the spring and
summer that followed, I ran into fellow competitors who, as
the jargon ran, were "going up" that fall, or, worse, the elect
preparing for their second or third year "in residence." I
longed to go up, with all that phrase's hint of aerial promo-
tion, and to be in residence would be enclosure in a commo-
dious trance. Furtively, at soccer or cricket matches, I perused
the foreheads of the chosen few, eventually deciding that the
typical winner's brow was low, concave, and signed with three
undulant creases, whereas my own, impassive mirrors proved,
was high, bulged slightly, and bore no lines at all. In a desperate effort to make the mind conform, I incised three magical cicatrices above my eyes with the round end of a nail file,
admiring the look of distracted maturity I thought they con-
ferred, until the skin regained its natural tension and I became
an also-ran again.

Slogging away at books in my third-story bedroom, at a
table to whose overvarnished top my elbows stuck fast, I ran
the gamut of affronted aspiration, certain I would glide in au-
tomatically next time provided, say, I wore an olive-green
shirt, or looked paler than Banquo's ghost. A more pragmatic
magic, however, set me poring over paperbound volumes of
past examination papers (though I shrank from looking in the
back at those in whose presence I had betrayed myself last
year). Within those ferrocyanide-blue covers lay the keys of a
genteel kingdom, perhaps in the compulsory translation from
Latin (*how* could Tacitus's *"temptat clausa,"* bald brace in a
museum tongue, mean all of "he tried to open all the closed
doors"? Was this to be my own motto, malefically secreted
among the stuff of my undoing?). Or was it in the three-hour
general essay paper ("Discuss logic," or " 'The unexamined

life is not worth having.' Consider.")? Who was I to opine on logic, expert that I was in muddle, especially after grappling with Bertrand Russell's *The Problems of Philosophy*, in which all chairs became unreal fascii of qualities? As for the unexamined life, I knew only, from recent bitter ordeals, that it might actually be an unmitigated joy (no more three-hour essays) and that, in a less shallow sense, although the unexamined life might not be worth having, the examined one might not be worth living.

In nightmares I kept meeting pimply geniuses with narrow, sunken, striated brows, who jubilantly remarked on the easiness of the translation from Chinese, the piece of cake the literary history paper had been (mad minutiae pincered from a continuum rolling from Homer to Halldór Laxness), and the trivial stimulus of even the hardest essay topic ("Discuss any teleology implicit, or seemingly so, in the categorical imperative"). The only consolation, idle gossip of school cloakrooms, was that these examinations were stiffer than the universities' own final degree papers; graduates (oh, what Prometheans!) had repeatedly said so, and the dons (noetic pharaohs) concurred. Almost broken on the wheel when young, the winners breezed through the ensuing three years as if playing snap. Into the bargain, if bargain there would ever be, I came from a secondary school, which sounded downright second-class (although it only denoted post-primary), not a grammar school (where they syntactically and strategically meant business), and still less a public school, meaning private, which as often as not had closed scholarships available to its own boys only. Besides, *we* had girls on our premises, which surely proved the school's essential lack of high seriousness. I envisioned a hypothetical secondary scholarship, available only to our school, and then dreamed up the deaths—by traffic, pneumonia, and brainstorm—of my immediate rivals, at length accepting my award with the smile of a fireball coming home to roost.

Studying previous papers, those libretti of past inquisitions, I marveled at the arcane trophies to be had. As well as open scholarships, which explained themselves, there were the aforementioned closed ones, restricted to Etonians, descendants of King Canute, or anyone born west of a line drawn from Berwick-on-Tweed to Land's End, but also indiscreet or painterly-sounding exhibitions, wholly enigmatic sizarships, with faint connotations of glue or paste, and bisected things called demyships, for which one perhaps received only a half-stipend. Lowest of all were commonerships, at which I now set my cap. Of such illustrious colleges as Cambridge's King's, which may have been only for male royalty, and Trinity, only for the devout or those who thought in threes, or Oxford's Magdalen (what if one whorishly mispronounced it during interview?), and Balliol, which was full of invincibly brilliant Scotsmen who thought all night in calculus, I had no hopes. In fact, I was addressing my endeavors to St. Catherine's and Selwyn Colleges, Cambridge, combined, and St. Edmund Hall, Oxford. Amazing as it now seems, not every college offered an examination in English Literature, almost as if, compared with the intricate preliminaries of Medicine, Literae Humaniores, or what Cambridge forbiddingly termed Moral Sciences, it weren't a serious subject at all. Anyone worth his salt knew it backward and would not persist with anything so ephemeral; but for secondary-school boys it might just do, like them having come so recently into being, an upstart lit. for an upstart lot.

So I forgot Oliver Cromwell's college and, to equip myself with a unique, local angle, began to study the poems of Edith Sitwell. Not daring to present myself for interview at the portals of haunted Renishaw Hall, I schooled myself in village gossip, amassing gaudy yarns of Edith's ring-encrusted hands, her habit of sleeping in a coffin in ornate robes, her basilisk's eye, her Plantagenet nose like a molten string bean, the iron mask she had been forced to wear as a child. Opening the local flower show on St. Peter's cricket ground, where I had often flung red leather balls at clay-brown stumps, she looked like some hopelessly etiolated macaw, not of this aviary at all but rented for a fee to be paid in Erewhon orchids. Fervently I worked out close analyses of her most sensuous poems, evolving bogus theories (if indeed the expression itself is not tautologous) of verbal enamel and the annular baroque, identifying at a class-conscious distance with her exotic aloofness, and even going so far afield as to rehearse little monologues on Sacheverell Sitwell's poems, Osbert's slapdash use of the dash. A contribution to knowledge it was not, but it *was* viaticum and exam fodder in one. After a few months immersed in *Façade* and *Gold Coast Customs*, our man from Renishaw was ready for the Goliath brains of next December's inquisitors. This time, although the two examinations almost overlapped, there would be no sixteen papers in six days (which had meant three papers on four) but, in either place, a civilized new-style trivium of Authors, Periods, and General, to be followed by an interview, at which one stood a fair chance of being incompletely exhausted. Oxford came first, then I had to go, via Bletchley Junction, where Franz Kafka was reputed to have lived in the signal box, to Cambridge, a tricky cross-country trip: from the patrician matrix of prime ministers to the sagest old clinic of the midcentury.

St. Edmund Hall was a tiny place just off Oxford's thunderous High Street, where University College and others were subsiding an inch each year owing to the vibration from traffic and, some decades thence, would disappear from view into a Dark Ages compost that no doubt included the bonemeal of Oxford's eponymous ox. The formulas of arrival did not vary markedly from those of what Oxford men referred to, with jocular hauteur, as "the other place"; yet it was a serious jocularity, and what Oxford respected in its less fruity sibling was a medieval childhood held in common. Arriving at the porter's lodge, one was put into the custody of a "scout," who, presumably knowing his way through the Mohicans and Comanches of the academy, conducted one to yet another set of temporary rooms, whose absent tenant had his embossed calling card set in a little brass frame let into the oak, as the outer door was called. To be private here, for whatever purpose, you locked the outer door, known as sporting the oak. Needless to say, I sported mine as soon as I could, and took out my last-minute notes.

Furtive, voluptuous comparisons, however, strayed through my concentration. After all, I would be off to Cambridge in a couple of days. Cambridge gowns were voluminous, those of Oxford mere rectangles with ribbons. At the former, one was catered for by a "bedder," an appellation whose venereal-maternal overtones reinforced themselves in the fact that some bedders were female. Oxford had no female scouts, however, and I detected, I thought, generalizing wildly on too narrow a base, a magistral teak on the scout that bedders lacked: a minatory politeness which proved who really ran that ancient seat of learning, whatever its Hebdomadal Council thought.

My bedroom overlooked the college cemetery, an oblong trap of headstones and curbs all at conflicting angles, as if scrambled by a minor earthquake. I thought of Paul Nash's wartime painting *Totes Meer*, in which fragments of airplanes canted up from the bowels of a lugubrious marsh to recombine

themselves into a Frankenstein flying machine: a Junkerschmitt
17, say, or a Focke-Dornier 109, which as the last trump
sounded would bombard us all over again, this time with tons
of methane-heavy magma. St. Edmund's graveyard threatened a like resurgence, its composite outcome a giant Latin-
booming head on a sketchy trunk, come to repel boarders
from the uncouth north. I shivered for all three days; the tiny
hall stood over an icy meer, I guessed, and the little electric
fire in my sitting room warmed only the peeling frame. Yet
the magic of old Oxenford prevailed: one came here precisely
to be cold, for cold made the mind adept. The only hot water
of the day arrived in a tin jug with the scout at seven A.M. and
poured from a kettle at teatime. "Gently with the gas, sir, and
the power," he said, as if advising how to handle two beloved
artifacts. "The *austerity*, you know." Certainly no south wind
frolicked in his voice. It was 1947, year of a feral, embattling
winter such as I never again saw until, a decade later, I discovered January in Montreal. The little kitchen reeked of
grease, gas, and mouse dirt, but it was Cathay to me. Some of
the headstones I perused were of the fourteenth century. I had
taken a train right into history, a train that did not stop and
had no terminus; no matter how many times you changed, it
bore you on, then dropped you off while other passengers
went gratefully ahead.

Awed, and with chattering teeth, my mind intoning a round
based on the title *Aula Sancti Edmundi*, I ran into Vice-
Principal Kelly, a forbiddingly tall, aquiline-faced theologian,
whose handshake descended diagonally from a black-clad altar six feet high. It was like shaking hands with St. Patrick
himself, except that this saturnine young cleric spoke in impetuous diphthongs about having just played squash, of which
game I had never heard, even though I played it later on and
became almost proficient. I had never met such jovial fellows

in my life, not even those who rented out donkeys at the seaside or massacred rabbits in the Sitwell woods, and could only
conclude that these sublime luminaries—*fellows* indeed—who
ran colleges were forever either ill-suppressing convulsions of
mirth at the awkward antics of examinees or tuned in to some
acerb transubstantial farce. One inadvertently looked around
for the master of the revels, in the dreadful iron-clanging,
earthenware-cisterned lavatories, in the staircase tunnels that
led from quad to quad (or court to court), even in the examination room itself, where the scouts of St. Edmund continu-
ally stoked up and fussed over a fire that had no right to be
indoors: a Dickensian conflagration that made one long for
the moment when the doors opened and someone said, "Gen-
tlemen, you may begin." One literally warmed to one's task
as, outside in the cold, young men still in residence even during
vacation coughed and joked on their way across the quad in
bulky red-and-yellow scarves.

This time around, my state of mind had shifted through a
degree or two of arc: the intoxication was there still, but less
with the chance to show off, to kick over the Gradgrind traces,
than with the opportunity to sit and write about the things
that delighted me in my heart of hearts. No examination as
such, this was an invitation to further enchant the converted:
a swelled-headed reading of the circumstances, to be sure, but
one that precluded tyro's nerves and found me, I recall, smiling
complacently at the foolscap as each examination began. The
Fellows of the Colleges wanted to know what I knew and
could do, I told myself, and not what I didn't or couldn't. That
civilized affirmativeness drew me out into a phalanx of rip-
pling, ill-juxtaposed sentences in which I somehow conveyed
my unique stance on the Sitwells, my modified astonishment
at Plato's famous divided line, and, preposterous as I now find
it when I think of the predominantly literary context, my nym-

pholeptic air-mindedness, all the way from Daedalus to Sir Frank Whittle's jet engine. A youth of fragments who might not grow into a man of parts, I acquitted myself with a confidence I had been obliged to invent. And then, along with several other candidates, I entrained for Cambridge, an old hand on that battlefield, I reckoned, vaingloriously reassuring myself that, if all else failed, I was the only one of them who had played cricket for his county's Boys. Surely Derbyshire sporting prowess would win the day should the lowdown on the Sitwells fail. I dashed a few lines home on letterhead I was not entitled to, in an envelope enhanced with St. Edmund's arms.

Weird as it felt, I was beginning to know my way round colleges. Such familiarity would never be allowed to go to waste. Again porridge, beans and bacon, marmalade and cupric-tasting tea, began our day. Burned, flour-costive soup and vile beef curry, followed by jam tart, were the lunch. Pipsqueak ironists, we protested our conviction that England had *won* the war, not lost it, so why the frontline rations? One boy produced a cherrywood pipe and lit it, biliously intense. We all dashed out for postcards and little handbooks to the colleges. A London candidate actually purchased the college's tie, which our Oxford contingent thought a bit thick, though just as sure of ourselves as he. We invested shillings in gifts at one remove, those of the tourist rather than the rightful occupant: mugs ablaze with shields and unglossed Latin, calendars of punts on the river and daffodils on the Backs, frangible spoons with runcible lozenges of heraldry soldered in misalignment to their tops.

It rained each day. There were, of course, no daffodils. We poled no punts. The college was eerily still, a bell jar for wood smoke and the reek of boiling greens. I bought a big map of Cambridge and eyed the jet-black plan view thereon of Oliver

Cromwell's college, but stayed away. I felt a gathering sense of being in the midst of what the Greeks called *kairos,* seasonal time as distinct from mere chronicity. A thousand perceptions added up to fifteen sentences an hour, penned oblivious of clock or question. I wrote what I had come there to write, engraving the tablets before me with a horrendous mixture of gossip, purloined epigrams (just one of my own, which began, "The annals of anguish belie themselves"), and quotations learned by heart and fist and squeezed through the cheesecloth of critics whose true vocation, I later saw, should have been horology.

Who, T. R. Henn, the Yeats expert, asked me at my interview, was Tully? I babbled parabolical guesswork, slouching towards Cambridge to be born. Tully—was—*Cicero!* Had I *read* any Cicero? With blinking frustration I had, puzzled by a vehicle that so much competed with its tenor; had not Cicero's head and right hand been put on public view by Antonius? But this was sailing too near the wind; I reverted to my Yeatsian *moutons,* then dodged sideways into Edith Sitwell's *Gold Coast Customs,* a Byzantium of the aorta. . . . The kind and keen man cleared his throat but let me flow, and what happened after that I scarcely remember. A paralyzing ecstasy set in. St. Edmund's had telephoned St. Catherine's, as if through some interdenominational holy line. I had to choose, Henn said: if Cambridge, it would have to be Selwyn College, because it was Selwyn's turn (some such rigmarole). To ecclesiastical, red-brick Selwyn I walked, choked with mystery, but in the end chose St. Edmund, perhaps because of that ancient graveyard, or lofty Kelly in his dog collar, or those vast fires they built you to write by.

The impossible had happened. Then the possible erupted. There would be a mandatory two-year delay. While I did my military service, returning veterans would complete their interrupted studies, and then I could take up my scholarship. There was no way round it; the rule held at both places, and, it was suggested, a couple of years in uniform made a boy into a man as well as into a maturer student. But, having tasted ambrosia, I wanted a steady diet of it; I wanted to become not a man but a student, and an immature one at that. So I made what was then a sickening decision, almost as bad as going military: I settled for a provincial university, on an award I never even competed for but which came like a free sample in the mail after I passed a routine exam. Not quite my own executioner, but feeling every inch my own pawnbroker, I one day took the train to Birmingham, and three years later kept my appointment with Oxford, not in St. Edmund's *aula* after all, but in the college, Lincoln, that unleashed John Wesley on the pagan world. Anticlimax it surely was, yet one loaded with procrastinated joys. It began one of the happiest times of my life, perhaps because, once installed, I did next to no work at all, having done it, as it were, before arrival, during a succession of radiant summers whose uninsistent fleecy clouds partnered in my mind the blackened margins of innumerable books and print that swam and jigged until I knew not page from sky. I had flown blind through books, had learned the clouds by heart, confusing knowledge with magic, as always. Not facts but the fingerprints on them were my obsession; or, indeed, the etching of the whole palm: whorls, forks, asterisks, semiquavers, and scalpel-sharp crescent moons; or even, after overzealous chiromancers of the eighteenth century, the signatures or planets of our feet, which, facing earth, receive the weakest light and dwell, according to one Fludd, in a microcosmic night. An additional source of delight was that I remained still unclaimed by the military; what on earth, I wondered, would I have been useful for in Korea?

How stably you go home again, in your mind's eye unerr-
ingly plant a love tap at first base. The aerie room in which I
studied looks out still at a golf course where, during winter
floods, Gerald White, my grandfather's major domo, drowned
while saving a sheep. My school books are there, like empty
oxygen cylinders, dusted off by my mother the same day each
week, in case I ever need them again, need to start over. No,
that room is a bit of a shrine for a mostly absent son. The gilt
on the spine of the *Short History of English Literature* has
wanned beyond bleach into invisibility; the cover of my pocket
selection of French verse from Ronsard to Valéry has given its
friendly cobalt-blue back to the pouring afternoon sun; Russell's *Problems* falls apart if moved, into tiles of pages dangling
from glue-faceted threads that set the teeth on edge; the damp-
warped *Boy's Own Astronomy Handbook* still tells the truth,
sidereally reliable although written before the Hiroshima
bomb. I can still, thank goodness, lean my elbows on the
sticky-topped table and peer again at the black-and-white photograph of the globular cluster M 13 in Hercules, scintillating
eight inches and twenty-two thousand light-years from my ret-
inas. M 13's electric bull's-eye of spattered light, a boy's rune,
awes again, anachronistically crinkling like silver paper in a
match's flame. Yet it has a humdrum counterpart on our own
planet: not the photograph in my old album, but one of those
miraculous patterns traced by programmed worms. Fuzzy as
the state of mind in which I competed for my sweet tomorrow,
this pattern's winning caption says, after a number: cloud path
generated by a gentle worm.

10

WORDPLAY

Nines into Tens

I had just been through one of the most glorious passages
of my mother's music; she had scored it if not conducted it,
and I had been her soloist, coached and sponsored. But I had
been obliged to go away to do it. To get away you had first
to manage an almost symbolic going-away feint. Then you
came back, bearing the thing she wanted you to have without
having it: a kind of internal emigration that would transform
you without any more trains. I think she thought she would
lose me forever as I became encased in some silken berth of
smart-ass privilege. All through the examinations I had felt her
bright amused eyes sampling what I wrote as I told myself I
was doing it for me, for her, for her through me, fudging up
my own form of grateful vicariousness. This canceled Africa,
surely, and my father's being blinded. For once we were get-

ting a bit of honor back, or, if not honor, then reward. Did it cancel her blighted music career as well? I was taking everything upon myself, making even the bravest phrases responsible for too much. *Is it not easier to die than to live?* I remember writing with Victorian pomp, thinking that wasn't a bad way to start an essay on the deceits of cheerfulness, but not even so sonorous a phrase could shoulder the domestic freight I put upon it. Sure, you did it to show the examiners, like Cocteau with Diaghilev, and to get some obscure payback, but you did it mostly for love of language, infatuation with a birthright. Much later, I met a poet who said the trouble with winning things is that the people you most wanted to please by it were no longer there.

In much the same way, to write about that Oxbridge suite and variations conspicuous in what I am calling her music was to some extent to do without my mother, not mentioning her for pages at a time, for me writing now, rather than the teenaged me writing the examinations in a preoccupied fever, a nagging pain. I brighten, though, because, gentle monitor, she is always there, with a voice of strict spiritual delicacy. Writing those exam papers, I was learning a new language: that of the absence within autonomy, Spartan and caustic.

It must have been about this time, amid the jubilation and the anticlimax, that I first heard of a distinction between art and life, as if they were separate. Art was for weaklings, life for heroes: something crass was in the air, an aftersmog of war. A mid-1950s French version would eventually damn the *nouveau roman,* that masterwork of obsessive philatelical doodling, as cowardly compared to the naked existentialism of the Resistance. Such distinctions done subtly or otherwise have always made me uneasy. They were there in the grammar school, as in the main girls plumped for arts and youths for sciences. To do as I had done increasingly, along with one other, Derek Wilkinson, struck the sixth form as timid. Even the girls we joined thought so. It was as if we had swapped the Resistance for fiddling while Rome burned. Fired by such prejudice, I began to increase my devotion to the arts and things arty, firmly backed by my mother, to whom life was seamless, but getting looks of wry chagrin from my father, who, however, didn't make an issue of it—so long as he did not have to pay. My mother's maxims helped a great deal. It wasn't enough that, at school, I got away with my artistic pretensions because I was a doughty cricketer; I wanted to feel intact in my own mind, and vindicated. Had I realized then how much toil a so-called artistic career entailed, especially that of the novelist, I might have risked my mediocre math and tried my hand at aircraft designing. Not that I thought the artist's life that of a fop. I hadn't thought much beyond an addiction to literature and a subsidiary role as a teacher, which of course came about.

My mother knew I was immersed in an unstable element in which I might flounder and drown. Many had. Many do. Yet I vaguely knew, from her guidance, that something deep inside would save me, and her reasoning had merit: if I had had enough drive to get through the early stages—the examinations and the interviews in which I tried to fish something unique out of my dead center—I might just manage to have such a career as she had once begun. She knew all about the uphill first years, when everybody would rather you did something else, and she knew the answer lay in some inward operation of the spirit, a voluptuous goading of one's gift until, hey presto, somebody said, Well, there's something there; it may not last a lifetime, but it's bonny. *Bonny* was the village's non-sissy word for lovely, exquisite, handsome, beautiful: nobody wanted these things to vanish, but nobody wanted to be heard extolling them in fancy language either. A bonny lass

was a girl so desirable that no one could bear to look at her
or think about her, so extreme were people's responses.

Having said that, however, I begin to wonder all over again.
True, *bonny* was good-looking, but I think it also signified
something vague. You said it, now and then, when you weren't
willing to commit yourself to lovely, beautiful, perfect, not out
of shyness but out of near-disapproval. Bonny was sometimes
good enough, and I do recall people's taking offense at being
called no better than bonny, which might conceal fatness, or
crudity of manner. All in all, it was a word best not used, even
though to me it had a lovely French flavor. It was better that
a shy-sounding compliment should not seem to hide a guarded
sneer. Called bonny myself, I knew that mingled in with the
praise and the pleasure went a reference to my chubbiness. *A
bonny little chap* was a phrase that could wound a tot. To an
adult, it was an outright insult; the smiler with the knife under
the cloak, or the cloaca, had doffed his coat.

When my mother said *bonny* she used it to praise. When
she had reservations, she kept her mouth shut, and her eyes
glazed over in studious neutrality. There were superlative
times, though—puddings, cakes, sweaters, Liszt played well,
stunning art—when she said *lovely, beautiful, perfect,* and you
knew you were in the presence of the unimprovable. Something extraordinary had happened, and an uncommon destiny
had erupted from the midst of a quite ordinary process. The
adored item had become a law unto itself, we thought, she
and I, surpassing all conventions and forerunners. I was being
initiated into the realm of beauty with appalling slowness, and
it was from my mother I learned eventually to try to make the
sentence in hand as good as I could before going on to the
next. Why move on, leaving monstrosity behind? I wish I had
managed to live up to that all the time, but you do not always
recognize a wart. I came to know that although you often

abandon a piece of work, you work on it until your mind aches. My mother worshiped work almost as much as she did beauty, and I do believe she had the worshiper's temperament, which, needing to venerate, will embellish the desired object until it becomes more than itself, no longer open to scrutiny. She had in her soul the makings of medieval courtly love, that figment of Platonic playtime. I too was all for converting nines into tens so as to have my self-induced shudder of delight in the presence of the magnificent. I had learned this too from Arthurian Tennyson and from Wordsworth the idolater of children.

Fuel for all this vagary, other than my mother's role as catalyst, came from dead Uncle Douglas's Netherthorpe Grammar School books. Now *that* was a real school, where grammar pounded into you day and night. As a metallurgist-to-be, he hardly needed grammar; indeed, soon to be dead, he might have needed a crash course in living and dying. He had gone to Africa virtually engaged to Norwegian Ruth, fallen there for the boss's daughter, and then died of pneumonia. Now I had his books and his dusty collection of huge African butterflies and moths. I wondered how he had found time to collect them. As the wings gathered even more dust, on top of that from the veldt, but this time soot from the mining valleys of Derbyshire, I dipped into his anthology of French poems and found myself stunned by Sully Prudhomme's "Le Vase Brisé," a classic of sentimental symbolism. Like Uncle Douglas, Sully Prudhomme was a youth of faint health and pensive disposition. He won the Nobel Prize in 1901 when he was sixty-two, for being like Lamartine and Vigny; but I had never heard of that vaunted prize, nor of Sully's other works. I was just responding to his melancholic sensibility, of which I had more than a little myself, an odd quality to find in a rough-and-ready mining village. I also inherited Alexandre Dumas's

Histoire de mes Bêtes, "Edited By L. H. Althaus, Organizing Mistress in Modern Languages in the West Riding, Yorkshire." What a bossyboots she must have been. And there were several other Blackie's Little French Classics, bound in dungreen paper, uninviting as tarpaulin. I nosed my way into them anyway and reconfirmed my love for the French language, French literature especially. It was strange with my mother raising me on the English classics and my young dead uncle on the French ones, the one still hoping to deflect me into music, the other's butterflies and moths awaiting my clumsy attentions. Patchy as my vocational reading was, while I waited for university life to begin, it was unusual, and I had that superb ticket of leave: I could quit school whenever I wanted to and was just luxuriously marking time in the sixth form, getting in my cricket and soccer as a young jock should, gabbing with Pauline Fisher* and Isobel Walker, and delving into what my teachers with a sniff or two wrote off as Romanticism, especially that of Rousseau. I had become what schoolmates called a swot: one who hits the books far too much out of sheer affinity and cryptic ambition, but so what? Who were *they?* The underprivileged of years to come. I was far too pleased with myself and needed to be thrown again into the holly bushes to learn humility. I read on and on, and began to write poems, none of which I showed to my mother, though she finally saw them in a university magazine and found them "dry."

---

* An enthusiast wrote to me only the other day saying she had handed my novel *The Place in Flowers Where Pollen Rests* to her literary mentor in Los Angeles, who said, oh, she went to school with him and remembered him carrying his cricket bag on weekends. Pauline Fisher, who won the medal for spoken French, *remembered* and then wrote to me, explaining that the enthusiast whose mentor she was happened to be her own daughter. What a tease time is.

A Village Vocabulary

Ever practical, she worried about my weird eating habits. When I was away from home, what would I live on? The only food I liked was eggs with bacon and fish with fries, plus chocolate cake. I have a nephew with the same lethal tastes. I would never eat greens or crusts, fruit or beets or turnips. It has always been thus, despite my mother's attempts to lure me into a balanced diet. One of the ironies of my life has been at last coming to broccoli, spinach, Brussels sprouts, and cauliflower, only to be forbidden them because crucifers, rich in potassium, interfere with the anticoagulant I take. So hail, greens, and farewell. These days, I am also forbidden carrots (they boost the blood sugar too fast) but medically exhorted to eat yams, sweet potatoes, and other orange things, all of which I loathe. Thank goodness for corn, peas, and chickpeas.

Detecting in me the onset of decadence, quickly followed by indigestion, Mother tried to put me on the straight and ample path to health, but it was not to be. Her major triumph was to make me eat a huge bowl of porridge every morning laced with molasses and followed by a tablespoon of cod-liver oil. What dreaded diseases she thus saved me from I can't imagine. At least her boy stopped blinking; puberty had come and gone, and certain touchy sexual matters she left to my father, who ignored the whole thing as banal and tedious. The only advice he ever gave me, he who had just about survived the First World War, was to buy a good pipe and then, whenever I felt low, "all of you draining into the pit of your stomach," smoke it with a nice strong drink at hand. Thus my father's version of the birds and the bees. Sex, it seemed, had much to do with depression. He may have been right, for himself at least (though not as I willfully depict him in *Love's Mansion*: a blind Lothario). I think my mother was quite explicit with my sister about menstruation, but that was woman-to-woman, whereas the legendary man-to-man did not exist for me. I was going to be a transplant, my first undertaking a crash course in Greek: just what I needed to acquit myself well in the twentieth century. I was also reading modern Greek poets in translation, drawn most to Cavafy and Seferis. I was preparing for yet another unpragmatic phase, the very antithesis of my mother's famous brothers—two metallurgists to make the steel, one butcher to sharpen it.

My highfalutin enterprises went on in a keenly verbal house. We were word people as well as music people. With what avidity we seized upon the speech defect of a neighbor girl who said "Nes" for "Yes." We *nes*sed together all day with ungenerous giggles, mispronounced *fish* as *fush* and *teach* as *feech,* just for the licentious prank of it, and even called a certain fish-shaped candy *fix mishtures* instead of *fish mixtures.* This was the relief of virtuosi, I suppose, guying language because we had it firm within our grasp. So *hello* became *ewwoe, just* became *jutst,* and *missus* (or Mrs.) became *mitits.* So it was possible, if the occasion presented itself, to say, "Ewwoe, Mitits Fush," though we never did. Baby talk had met an older bedlam, in which *hand* became *handle* and *foot fussy.* It was revenge, in a way, on the village argot that baffled outsiders with *shant* (place), *clart* (mess or muck), and *spadger* (chewing gum). Even worse for the uninitiated was the accent, which mutilated familiar words almost beyond recognition: *redlar* for *regular, neet* for *night, ooam* for *home, corsey* for *causeway* (sidewalk), and so on. The word *you* was scarce, having yielded to a weird succession of Quaker-sounding *thee*s and *thou*s with local variants such as *thĭ* (yours or thy) and *thā,* a corruption of *thou.* Yet there persisted an old shibboleth against misuse of the second person singular; villagers knew it had once upon a time, before *you* bit the dust, been a special form of address, for use among intimates. Why, the French have a verb for using *tu* with people: *tutoyer.* Well, we had no verb for it; but an assumption, a discrimination, remained. I once heard an aggrieved wife outside a pub berating her husband, who had obviously said something like "Thee, tha wants to shurrup." "Don't *thee,*" her retort went, "*thou* me, thou *tharrer!*" He was being too familiar, in language at least. My mother enjoyed this dialect-and-accent zoo. Knowing that the local mode of speech was crude and uncouth, she nonetheless sometimes settled into it with an antic, elfin smirk, slithering down the ladder of propriety sans blemish. When my sister and I did the same, she took offense and chided us for letting the side down. All such locutions, or vagaries of speech, passed my father by completely; he was the most correct speaker of the four of us, still a sergeant making himself clear to men with accents and brogues of all kinds. He could never see the point of regional yawp; it had no use and no charm, so he just shrugged at our foolings with English and got on with his newspaper; none of *that,* his intentness seemed to say, in language nobody could fathom. Wordplay was a joy, however, especially to me, who could see the exuberance in naming, hear the old language-builders in my own throat, honing a mumble into a word. Some of my mother's denunciations, though, came right from the dictionary. "A proper muddle!" she would exclaim. Then there were shadings: "You daft thing!" And a silly person she would call "a right Herbert," I have no idea why. I should have compiled a village vocabulary for later use, but I never did; my mother bore it in her head, and I knew she would last forever.

11

THE LOWDOWN
ON THE UNIVERSE

A Midnight Flit

One late-August evening, we sat in the gray armchairs, commending the way the light lingered—we saw less of the dark that led to the morrow. Or so it seemed. Without warning, other than rhetorical, my mother began to talk of something else. "I've been thinking," she said, "I'd like to leave Eckington and move to Empingham, to be nearer to Sheila." It was not a new idea, but fondness for her maisonette had put it on the shelf. Now, however, there seemed some urgency. Not many phone calls later, with all the things she treasured stashed in a couple of suitcases, she turned her back on Eckington, where she had lived for ninety years, and never mentioned its name again. Not even her friends knew she was leaving, never to return; accustomed to seeing her take off for a week or two, they hailed her departure with a wave and remained glad the

world was full of habitual things. My mother slept all the way
as my sister's husband Bill threaded an economical course at
about eighty-five miles an hour southeastward through Nottinghamshire into Leicestershire and so to Rutland, the small-
est county in the country. I thought of how, after Beatrix
Potter's death, her bereaved husband left her things where they
were, including a bar of chocolate on her worktable, half-
eaten, with her teethmarks evident on it. From things about
to disappear, you turn away.

When my mother arrived, she awoke, at ease; after all, as
she often said, she had slept in every one of the rooms in my
sister's house, even the dining room, and knew a room always
awaited her. She had done what Derbyshire called a midnight
flit, from a village where she was famous to one in which she
knew no one but Tranquil Gaunt, another music teacher,
whose name suggested only just reconcilable qualities. The
main thing, it struck me, was that Mother had made good her
escape, soon after making one of her most apocalyptic re-
marks, said offhandedly for effect: "I have been *a woman* for
almost one hundred years." That impressed and pleased her,
I could tell; she could speak with continental-sized authority
now. So here she was, transplanted into familiar turf—a village rather more genteel than the other one, less riotous, less
animated by beer, not a mining but a farming village, and a
dormitory for Leicester executives.

After a month or two, she moved into a bed-sitter with some
few of her possessions, having selected a new carpet (indeed,
at one point she sat on the roll of it in the store, looking wholly
stranded and profoundly fed up). Too much moving had
"maddled" her, as she said; she wanted to watch TV for a
week or two and cook some of her own meals, quietly and
slowly. She had moved into an attractive, bright apartment
house in which the young and the old affably mingled. There

was a central quadrangle, grassed over like that of an Oxford college, and a community room with magazines, games, and a piano. This last attracted her not at all, but, as soon as she landed, there were rumors that she would play for them and, indeed, teach. What a preposterous idea, she said; her playing days were done. Her hands were numb, and not all of her furniture had arrived. She had heard such rumors before, when on holiday by the sea, and she was going to refuse, as always.

She was missing Jean, her Italian-looking neighbor back in Eckington (Jean had looked after her with the dogged zeal of a follower), but she was making new friends already, first of all Rikki, once a Dutch refugee from Hitler, who lived opposite her; then a wiry alert small man who, at a certain point, having tired of being someone else, had changed his name to one he'd heard and fancied (Reyner Rilka). There was also the Scots warden of this mixed college, Mrs. Annie Muir, a rosy-faced sociologist whom my mother soon began to call Heart of Midlothian. In no time, my mother, a good gabber after shy beginnings, was telling them all about the nineteenth century, "before almost anything," and making a fetish of introducing just about anyone as "my dearest friend." It looked as if she and her invisible orchestra of goodwill would soon be taking over. She got quite oratorical, maybe for practice: "Have you met my dearest friend Reyner Rilka, who lives here too?" At these moments of crossing the bar or stepping out, she achieved what looked like combustible lightness: an uncanny silver moved through her eyes, and she almost seemed to rise in the air, jubilant that her old good nature was coming back from the sentry boxes where dead bones moldered and steel mattresses bit into your back like early-model chest expanders. Rikki always told about the no-good RAF pilot she had married and left, but Reyner Rilka could be quite brilliant. He had once told her, and Mother, that the sound of antlers clashing in some TV documentary had sounded like billiard cues being rattled together. My mother thought this worth remembering and passing on to her son the novelist. I tried it. Reyner was right. I tried it backward, of course. How many things in the world, Reyner wondered, sounded alike? And why? Before the sun fried the earth, all things would sound alike, he said, amusing my mother, who told him nothing would ever sound like a piano, though she could tell some tales about pianists who had to have hair spray squirted on the keys lest their hands slip, and those whose hands perspired so much that their fingers skidded all over the place, never mind how much hair spray had been applied.

"You might get a tune or two, then," Reyner said, "out of somebody's hairdo." He kept her going, a jester, or a tart Fool, appealing to the side of her that said she was old enough to laugh the universe out of countenance, it had done so many terrible things to her already. I was delighted she had moved from a sustaining routine, with some callers, to the airy give-and-take of the hallways; she had moved into a population that actually welcomed me too, offering the spare room. At the same time, she was harping on death, the need to die. "I'm frightened, I really am. If I could only take you and Sheila with me, it might not be so bad. You love a little company." No soloist, my mother, bless her. This remark of hers upset my sister a good deal, but it seemed to me good gallows humor. My mother felt responsible for her children and did not want to leave loose ends behind her; so she would cart us along, then set up shop on the other side, where a decent piano or harpsichord might surely be had, and a cure for her agonizing back. She was willing to give recitals in the next world, even to teach, to make ends meet. Meanwhile, Flamingo would suffice; Reyner had thought of the name when someone asked him for one, and it had stuck, for most of the younger denizens anyway, not least for its having the word *flaming* in it. My mother, almost as soon as she moved in, proposed Gibraltar and Runnymede, but neither of these made it; nor did Avilion. Come to think of it, she added later, Flamingo is easy to say, except for those with speech impediments and short tongues. So Flamingo it came to be, for almost a majority (the word uttered never without a tincture of sarcasm and imminent buffoonery), while the rest simply called the place by its street address: 6 Rutland Court. Why the place had gone so long without a name or nickname, no one knew, but it soon became known among locals as *'Ave a flaming go,* alas.

One day while I was there, mingling and visiting (my mother never got used to the American use of this latter word to mean schmoozing), Rikki popped in from across the hallway with a small plant (impatiens, which my mother preferred to call by its other name, Busy Lizzie) and lingered to tell about the time her pilot ex had illegally taken her up in some type of plane and had done aerobatics so fierce that, when she got back to earth, her womb had sagged into her panties. She had given birth to her own uterus, and the incongruity pleased her still. It was almost as if, she said, she was being paid back for something: too much contraception, too much douche, too many abortions. My mother and I wondered how many, aghast to be confided in thus by a virtual stranger, then realizing it was only to strangers that people told such things. Intimates, to my mother, were folk you'd known for seventy years. Mustering all her poise, she exclaimed in one slow word after another: "Your—womb—in—your?" She could manage no more, and I thought how much at this point we needed that woman from Eckington, Mrs. Burdett, who always said, "if you understand me, Mrs. West." She, the doubting Burdett, could have aired our disbelief for us.

From now on, as if Mother did not have enough routine

excuses for not flying ever again (her first and second flights, between Liverpool and the Isle of Man, had delighted her, however, way back then), she could invoke Rikki's prolapse and leave flying to me and the NATO youths who thundered over only a hundred feet up in things called Tornadoes, their minds on a boy scout Armageddon. Rikki's womb in her panties had told her she could come seriously undone, not to be put together again. My mother reveled in Rikki's stories, though, preferring to hear them alone with her, then to recite them to me with a face of unforgiving shock.

At certain times, when my sister and I had taken precise notice of programs to come, we would arrange for Mother a stereo concert, tuning the TV and the radio to bring her the identical program (she watched the video usually) in an astounding mélange of sounds. She loved this oceanic duplication, looking around her in amazement at, so to speak, different parts of the orchestra, and I was again reminded of something special in her attitude to music: she knew there was always something beyond the performed music, the music as performed—a hinterland, say, or an extra dimension of which she heard samples now and then, but which she would never receive in its entirety. This open-endedness fascinated her, haunted her, reminding her of statements made in familiar piano pieces but detected only during her one hundredth performance of them. I reminded myself of one experiment of my own: setting up a bank of tape recorders to play all of Beethoven's symphonies simultaneously, with clotted, gnarled, insistent results. At the same time as trying to amplify her hearing opportunities, we tried not to overload her (she called it overfacing). Too much thunder in the speakers and she began to wilt and quiver, so we kept the volume down while surrounding her with sound. We were a long way from the old days of the piano tuner, plonking and clonking while her children giggled, or so-called jazz bands in the Eckington streets, bugling in black-and-white tunics.

The Safety of Troy

People sometimes ask me if I still hear my mother's voice, and of course I do. Usually she is saying, "That's the style!" —the phrase she used to honor something going right; or "Now then!"—used to awaken me if I was making a pig's ear of a worthwhile project. Or she is announcing that Winston Churchill saved Great Britain during World War II by inspired use of sonorous prose, fortifying through righteous bombast. He scripted everything, even his improvisations, which he cleverly made sound offhand and flubbed. Experts on the bicameral mind will explain that I confuse her voice with that of ancient epic heroes buried deep in my gray matter; but never mind, I hero-worshiped her anyway. A quiet voice, hers, infused nonetheless with a soprano of alarm, as if attuned always to the many things that could go wrong. I sometimes think of her as a Valérian, a disciple of Paul Valéry (without having heard of him), who wrote of the *implexe,* which is the raising to exponential maximum of whatever you have going for you. She hated waste, not least because she, the budding professional, had to settle for amateur status—her brothers needed attention, and then her ailing mother. She did not belong with all those sacrificed daughters who if they were lucky managed to sit out their years behind a modesty panel in a commonplace office. Nor among those refined women who, suffering from goiter, concealed it by winding thick black crepe ribbon around their throats, and who always seemed to form a secret society. One day, surrounded by them, I would see the ribbons loosen and huge eggs of protoplasm slump to the heartspoon, the slot directly under the chin. My mother was one on her own in a score of ways. She had the knack of talking amiably to people of all kinds; she would come alight instantly for them, bringing their light to life, then go about her business. I mean she was not a mouselady, my perverse term for the backroom bureaucrat, who seemed everywhere when I was growing up: not just in school, but in all the places we had to go to get anything signed.

In a way—and I am sorry if this sounds academic—she was like the Palladium, or Palladion, the sacred statue of Pallas Athene that, so long as it remained within the city, guaranteed the safety of Troy. She stayed put while her children went away, and that was how she preferred it. Perhaps she had the soul of an ancient Greek. She would chide me for working too hard, as she put it. "You worked hard as a teenager. Can't you take it easy now?" I explained that I loved the work, that I needed to do it to stay in my right mind, and she understood at once, knowing that work loved was the finest destiny in the world. From Pennsylvania or New York, I would call her every Sunday at 1:15 P.M., Eastern time, as over the years the reception improved. Our conversations were always much the same, formulaic and firm, all reassurance and echo. Some Sundays, because my timing was right, I would let her listen to a concerto or a piece of chamber music fresh from America, and over the Atlantic the music would pour, needing no gloss. When we resumed, our talk had that peculiar stranded quality I had also noticed after playing a tape during a seminar, and it took us some time to reestablish conversation as a valid means of exchange. I could always detect her state of health from her voice, and when she sounded hoarse and frail I would worry all week, ever willing to berate myself as the son who wandered off, hunting strange gods in foreign parts. Sometimes, mostly on holidays, I couldn't get through to her, and I fretted away because I knew that the instant we hung up she would switch to *Songs of Praise* on her television—the Sunday night evening service from assorted churches around the country—and sing all the way through as if she were one of the congregation. So I knew that if I didn't get through at one-fifteen, I had best wait half an hour, by which time—five hours later for her—she would be getting tired, too tired to manage a transatlantic call. Besides, she had, as she saw it, lost the fifteen minutes we had not been able to devote to our talk. For a while I recorded messages, really letters, on tape and airmailed them over; but she preferred the live sound, the simultaneous instant, the magic of undersea cable and, later, satellite, which made us uncanny neighbors, wasting time on exclamations at the tonic immediacy of things: no distortion, almost no time lag. A past mistress of timing, she knew how to talk transatlantic, allowing just enough pause for what she said to travel to me. I told her only happy things, and some of these prompted from her the blue-ribbon phrase "I'm properly over the moon." Faithful to our timetable, I called her from phone booths all over America, once a cumbersome act, but no longer. The phone unnerved her unless the call was a programmed one: she knew who, from where, and what about. Telephone surprises were just that: welcome, but taxing. She would have adored videophone, though she would have worried how much of her the caller would see besides her face.

She was a fetishist about privacy; in her Eckington years, still living alone and cooking for herself, she shut herself in with three bolts, just like a New Yorker, trembling from the exertion, but on guard with a carving knife or, by chance, a saucepan full of scalding water. Whoever was out there, Russians or Nazis, skinheads or con men, she was ready for them, because she had heard about ruffians who preyed on the aged, and in that geographical area. Nothing happened. She introduced me to her incessant daytime callers as "my big boy," and that was that: I was free to ignore them all as I filled tablets of yellow paper that rested on the underside of an old serving tray as I sat in re-covered armchairs the color of a camouflaged battleship. "Clever writing again," they would observe, and then retreat to the kitchen to discuss the day's doings. Other times, in an earlier house, I would set my yellow tablet between knife and fork at the fully set table and scribble away, knowing I'd have to type it all up when I got back to the States.

"I don't know how you think of it all," she'd say just about daily.

"Because I'm your lad, Missus," I'd answer, and that satisfied her without giving anything away. She had birthed this creature: that's what her face said, and she wondered at such monotonous behavior as mine, unable to fathom why I couldn't get it all said in one book instead of going on writing them with incomplete messages in them. Something like that haunted her, nagged at her tolerance; at least if you played the piano, those within earshot got the benefit, whereas writing was so silent, surreptitious. He might be saying *anything*. Only once did I inflict a typewriter on my parents, my sister having married and gone; it drove them crazy, a clatter-piano, once again indecipherable, and inhuman to the ear. That was me typing an early novel, *Alley Jaggers*, set in that same village. "What is it this time?" she would shout over the racket of the keys, but I never knew what to say. A good idea gone bad or mad. How say that to her?

The Privatest Thing of All

She was remarkably sensitive to feelings I had that I was a freak. Oh, I passed muster all right, because of the cricket and some much less imposing soccer, but I felt different, far too sensitive. Looking back, I think I was worrying about what I would now call mystical tendencies no doubt absorbed from Wordsworth: getting much more from plowed fields, the umber of horses with the sun on them, the smell of freshly squeezed-out milk. I spent longer on things than others did. I lingered hungrily when others zoomed by, eager for a routine destination. It was the same with books; I would read the same page again and again, taking it to pieces, wondering how it worked (if it did). This, I thought, was no way to succeed in life, though possibly a way to accumulate a thousand unique perceptions. I was wishing my birthright away, yet not for long. I had often seen my mother peering at a page of Beethoven or Chopin, looking for something special. Her tendency was always to seek out possible problems in playing, but she had this other side that took in and marveled at the structure on the page, the way the music was thus and not otherwise. Her old question—where had it come from?—must have occurred to her time and again as she played Beethoven, Chopin, and the others; not being a composer, she wondered at the creative process and, I chimed in to myself, the sensibility that put such artifacts together. We often chatted about this being different; she had always felt so, and she sensed the same thing in me as I pulled my act together, trying out rapturous lines in letters to girlfriends. They would write back chidingly, suggesting I was having a *very* emotional year; so I kept the whole sensation to myself, sometimes leaking it to Mother in rather clinical terms, although never mentioning neurosis.

I was finding individualistic magic in what I read at the time:

Dylan Thomas and Edith Sitwell (again), Henry Treece and David Gascoyne. If I felt on the periphery, these people were out of sight but bringing back ingots of luminous magnificence. It was the only way to be, and any risk entailed was worth it. My mother knew this, having paid in blood for her infatuation with the pianoforte. I had to be true to myself, she told me; and when I protested that self was a process, a conduit, she laughed and thought that a fine beginning. I longed for something within to be true to. How could you be true to a sensibility? If you were a fascist or a Catholic, you could be true to that. But how be true to a register of fine perceptions or to their instrument, the red-hot coal that Shelley spoke of in his *Defence of Poetry*? The answer came much later, in two stages, about which I told my mother, only to have her shake her head because I was getting in too deep. She had strict tenets of theory and harmony behind her and was uninclined to wobble, though Schoenberg beckoned her—she wished all his music had been like *Verklärte Nacht*. First, I discovered, you had to try not to falsify what came in through the unique doors of your perception. All right. The snag was that in the business of phrase-making (as I still am), you were entitled to modify a perception in order to accommodate a fine phrase, a sudden find. Since all art was artificial, you had to allow yourself a degree of artifice; you were not a mere reporter but a magical intervener. I thought of Thomas Gray, meticulously noting the flora in the court of Peterhouse, his Cambridge college, and conveying an aura of utter trustworthiness. Did Gray ever fudge because a brilliant *mot* had come to mind? Not so's you'd notice. Subjective tabulation, I told myself: that was the stuff, that was the role.

The second insight I had was that even if you fudged, you had added something to the sum total of created things. Nothing could fall out of the universe; therefore you were bound to have added, even if nobody knew what the addition was. It was up to you to declare it or not. My mother liked this proposition much more than the other one. She could always, a nontraveler, see the white wake of the boat cutting across Lake Something-or-other in the moonlight, her mind like almost everyone else's in thrall to the critic Rellstab's vision, inspired by the *Moonlight*'s first movement, of heavenly radiance bathing ocean waves—though we agreed the sonata might more sensibly be named the *Guicciardi*, after Giulietta Guicciardi, to whom it was dedicated. Beethoven himself called the work *Sonata quasi una fantasia*. Yet, I thought, Rellstab had achieved something by dubbing the sonata the *Moonlight*; even he. Then I saw what I was really talking about: there was something godlike in adding to the universe. This was being like Beethoven, who, developing no Bach-like ecstatic humility before the handiwork of the Creator, felt something godlike in himself. I had tuned in to his defiance. So too had my mother, in her gentler way, though she felt the Creator in the long run would take the credit for everything, for obvious reasons. Only something that fell out of the universe might be ascribed to some other being. I had always thought this mystical side of mine remained invisible except to my mother, but it was not so: those to whom I confessed it laughed and said it had been apparent for years. Oh, I said, this private relationship with the universe was the privatest thing of all. And then I thought of a line in one of T. S. Eliot's essays, suggesting that a man who joined himself to the universe had nothing else to hook onto and should get a life. That idea never spoke to me, since the universal starstuff informs us all, at least until a different stuff comes along. Anyone who spurns the universe after being born into it has turned away from the heat engine of wonder.

My mother plied me, as if I knew, with questions about

heaven: where it was, what it was like; and all I could tell her was that it was here and now, *being with her,* and that any life after death was identical except that it never ended. In that way we were together for eternity. She almost liked this desperate conceit, little knowing I had always thought the afterlife, so called, could never disappoint: if it existed, it existed; if it did not, then you never knew. I trod a devious path for her, both believer and skeptic. One of her friends had lost a son in the war, a radio operator in the RAF, but had been having conversations with him through a medium. (Perhaps wireless operators had special privileges in posthumous communication; virtuosi of the ether, they got through to their mothers more easily than airmen in other trades: a double perk—they "operated" in what they flew through.) What did I make of that? she asked in her impetuous, trusting way. I made nothing of that, but I knew Mrs. Morgan was Welsh and imaginative. I also saw what was behind the question: why had Uncle Douglas, the lost adored sibling whom my mother had brought up as a son, never come through with just a few words? Would he ever? Had he been one of those who vowed they would do their damndest to get through "from the other side"? He was not the type. More probably he would appreciate the good rest, the relief from always being handsome (he was), and being spared Africa's paradoxical climate, which cooked him and chilled him in the same day. He would know my mother no longer needed him; she had another son, who was battening on his old schoolbooks and playing cricket every bit as well as he had. I forget what I told my mother about Uncle Douglas, who introduced death into a family that had never thought about it before. He destroyed at least two of them by dying; his mother never got over his death, and my mother gave up her calling in order to be her mother's nurse.

Having visionary chats with my mother, I soon found myself fudging up theology and occult comfort. The death of one loved one was for that person to rest or repose before the arrival of the other loved one, and their subsequent reunion. In this, no doubt, I wasn't that different from the first Hindu or Buddhist dreaming up a satisfactory system, but I sensed fiction going too far. Death was a respite, I tried to suggest, but my mother gave me an old-fashioned look. Why should she not? Who was I to know? Clearly her orthodox Church of England (Episcopalian) beliefs were not giving her much support, any more than her old school colors would have done. She liked the idea of an interim during which the soul took it easy before eternal reunion (I like it myself), but she found the notion a little too convenient, a bit of a con to seduce her into thinking death was generous. If I had been an aircraft designer in the making, she would not have been asking me such questions at all.

One instance she gave me was impressive. Or so I thought at the time as she tried to think her way past the door that locked the truth away. If she cooked fish for us, she could never bear to eat any; the stench, she said, upset her stomach. So she would have a pork pie or cook something different. She thought God, a word she used with scrupulous diffidence, was like that with regard to the world. After creating it, God couldn't stomach any more of it. The whole thing struck him as a mistake, I said unwarily.

"Are you criticizing my cooking?"

"No, your cooking's champion."

She seemed glad to have a way out of the conversation. I pondered the idea of the absconded god, but found it vague; it would be the nature of a god, or first cause, to be distant, indiscernible, wouldn't it? The trick, as god-botherers said, was to lure God into the open, making divinity deal with you on a one-to-one basis. This mortal algebra, while giving a lift to imagination, was not healthy; it was all right for me to speculate, but not to impose the results on an impressionable matriarch who found the idea of death repugnant. Ultimately these discussions with her became acutely painful: because she had put so much trust in me, she expected me to *know*; she didn't need a cartload of well-turned metaphors, she wanted the goods, the lowdown on the universe. She had sent me to Oxford and Columbia to find out; or, rather, she had allowed me to slink off to these fabled places. Oddly enough, the Church-dominated Oxford of the Middle Ages or the nineteenth century would have been an ideal place in which to probe cosmic distress. Certainly the Church of England wanted the university as a plaything and an anteroom, but it also catered to minds hungering for guidance in nonsecular matters—much more than the pagan Oxford of my day. The censer had become an abacus.

It was no use telling my mother the great religions were as imaginary as Wordsworth's pantheism, and just as arbitrary as well. It would be devastating to tell her that billions of humans had lived and died, unable to confide to one another anything of cosmic value beyond, say, stoicism or traditional accounts of the afterlife. From all that living, we learn nothing about death and after. It was preposterous, but it was how the universe is made. Humans are creatures with a passion for unanswerable questions.

She wanted none of this. When Uncle Douglas died, she saw his face in the flames of the living-room fire, but that was only his last fizzle while going over, nothing like a genuine return from beyond. She had no doubt she'd seen him, but she knew about telepathy and believed in it, as do I (having seen it in action). She was looking for a divine apology, perhaps, or at least a word from Douglas that he was all right, though bored.

When her mother died of pneumonia, she took me to see her for the last time, laid out minus the steel spectacles that had always given her an intimidating glint. She was more frightening than ever now, hard as a poker. On the gaunt, unswerving brow I planted a final kiss, as ordered, then said my goodbye to someone I had hardly known. My mother's farewell was much the same, also to someone she had hardly known. "Goodbye, Mother," she said, trimly decorous, sealing a chapter of her own life. I cannot imagine what she was thinking, but she was unlikely to wish further communication. She was going through the motions honorably, convinced that her mother had gone to a better world, where she would never interfere with anyone again.

In those later conversations about the literal death penalty we pay, I hastened to add that my theories about loved ones and the death interval applied only to those in whom the love nexus was nigh perfect. The prospect of being bossed about by her mother, for all eternity, would have put paid to Mommy, as I sometimes called her. Conjecturally, she believed in a code of heavenly rewards. Not only that, though this took me a long time to grasp: she believed also in energy, which she knew did not fritter itself away, spilling out into the galaxy in wasteful sparks. No: it survived the body and surged ahead, fared forth, somehow forming itself into a discernible entity. Such a wonderful thing as energy would not just expend itself; energy did not have to rest, even if the body did. She had heard too that the soul weighed something. It had been measured as it left the dying hulk. This blend of positivism and *élan vital* appealed to me, and I seriously wondered if it would be too bad to spend the afterlife cruising the solar system as a free agent, fizzing away among low-voltage company. I did not mention this to her because I thought it would conflict with her conception of angels, about which I had not read enough.

Nor did I tell her about the day, in a kitchen in Cheshire, with no trucks passing outside, when the table I was sitting at jumped about five inches away from me, all in one go. My bed creaked and shook for no good reason. I knew I was being haunted by— energy, but not of the malign sort. I wondered if she had had similar experiences and was shielding me from them.

If I had had chance, would I have told her about the UFO I saw in 1995 while treading poolwater on a glorious October afternoon not long after her one hundredth birthday? Slow, spherical, silent, it cruised toward me, huger than any flying thing I had ever seen, glossy and about seven thousand feet high. No plane, no balloon, no chopper, certainly no satellite, it looked like two noses from old Boeing *Stratocruisers* mated together to create something bulbous and windowed. So far as I know, no one else saw it, nor did I report it; I swam for an hour in a trance after it suddenly did a vertical U-turn and vanished at colossal speed. Had I told my mother about it, she would have asked the right questions: Was it from God? Did it mean us harm? Whereabouts in the universe had it sprung from? Were these the dead, or the unborn, come to view us? She would have relished its volume and its shine, like the lover of apparitions that she was, but it would have jarred her cosmology, her sense of semi-safety among the unanswered questions. Yet, in an odd calendrical way it *was* hers, her birthday present, a bit late, but just what a fan of Tennyson's Excalibur would have relished. When you have just retired from something (as I did from university teaching), people expect you to get a bit daffy, but my friends have been mighty civil about my UFO so near my mother's birthday. Daffy I may be, but my aircraft recognition is still pretty hot, and I never saw anything even remotely like that lumbering globe of a greenhouse. My mother would have welcomed it with open mind, instantly at the helm, making minute harmonic corrections.

12

FLAMINGO

Good Nights

My mother and I were a dawdling duet who went outside for half an hour and peered at cows, noting dung-caked haunches and irregular horns, different timing in swishes of the tail. Or we stared at the Busy Lizzies, wondering why they did well on so little light. We had this habit of trimming the world about us of appetizing stuff until all that remained was vacancy, and then we situated a certain object amid the vacancy to see how it looked. Once, I said something like "We could last a thousand years and still have something new to stare at, something we hadn't looked at until then." She stared at me as if ready to chide, but smiled her most candid smile and told me what I never forgot: "We'll end up getting to know the inside of a wooden box. Just think how long you'll have to spend looking at that." It was even ambiguous.

"If you do," I murmured, stunned.

"Only if," I think she said. She was being terse. "You're right about that. Only if—that's about the size of it."

"Not with closed eyes," I added.

"You always get that." She sighed with enormous, taut gravity. "Doesn't it come with the suit?" She needed very little talk that year, content to sit there and sometimes hold hands, her numb one holding my partly numb one, but able to see the join and relish even what she could not feel. She had given up doing the crossword in her daily paper, and she took less interest in her TV, though it was new, whereas a few years earlier she had caustically characterized one sports performer as a greyhound, another as a polar bear, as if she saw all body contact in bestiary form. Now she let the players be themselves, exclaiming less, dozing off more, and sometimes forgetting if she had eaten lunch or not. After the huge upheaval of moving, she had become a devotee of the siesta, gradually, I thought, adjusting to geography an inch a day during sleep. Perhaps, in a phase of obtuse diffidence, she now intended a further flit, to a village where she knew nobody, and where, like an officer at war, she would make no friends so as to have no pain. Was that what she hankered for? No more pain. She attended no funerals but aimed little prayers for the dead up at the empyrean, thus soothing herself in endless survivorship. Where, I know she kept asking herself, had all the souls of all those people gone? Surely the universe would not waste them.

Each evening she said her farewell with regal awkwardness, not content to have me kiss her good night at the door of her apartment, on my way back to my sister's house. Taking up her stoutest cane, she made sure she had her key in hand before escorting me along the hallway that smelled of Gauloises, though I had never seen anyone smoking there. Perhaps you could buy the smoke bottled in Paris so as to generate a cozy atmosphere, as of a foreign airport. How *should* a Flamingo smell? When we came to the chairlift, as she called it, she sat herself in the chair, cane held before her in touch with her knees, then swung the cushioned arm down, leaned on it, and pressed the button for Rise, which she did, still smiling at the outlandish quality of so familiar a ride. Clattering upward, she arrived on the floor above, swung her legs around, and dismounted with an energetic sigh, facing the entrance hall, where you could pick up small bags of potatoes for ten p per bag. After a while she stood and did not advance until she was sure she had irrevocable control of her legs. She then conducted me to the main door, resisting my best efforts to cup her elbow. On rainless nights she actually stepped outside and stood there, breathing hard, mysterious and slight in the dusk as I faded from view, halted at the turn, stood waving as she brandished her cane, then half left, only to turn back again and wave afresh, after which there was nothing for it but to leave, although I never made a move until she had aboutturned and gone back inside, where, I was sure, she stood a while longer to be sure I wouldn't wave again. This could all take ten minutes as each waited for the other's final wave or gesture, neither able to trust empirical judgment and therefore waiting even longer, anxious not to be seen walking out on the other's last wave. How girlish her silhouette looked, how inappropriate the cane. She was using all her strength to do emphatic, punctilious things, never (she thought) knowing if she was going to make it through the night, though sure that *he* was the picture of health. Only in wars did you lose sons. She thus spent some weeks of each summer patrolling her destiny, guessing at finitude and fate only to find it postponed, obliging her to ponder a whole series of false alarms and ask what she had learned from a surfeit of reprieves—no, surfeit was too harsh a word; she would never look a gift reprieve in the mouth. Perhaps plenitude was the word for what the universe had in store.

She was still learning how to live, she said, sometimes reentering her hallway with a delighted chuckle at having made it to the outside world again. Both Rikki and Reyner had seen her do this, both of them habitually awaiting her return, looking out for her. Then, as she herself had told me, after a leisurely preparation she went to bed with her fate cuddled right beside her, for better or for worse, clad in one of the American nightdresses she had been saving until I insisted she wear them. She went to sleep in utter peace, as far as I could tell, knowing she had done all that could be expected of her that day, and dreaming if she could of her usual hearty breakfast, amazed still to be alive, even to have been born: meek and heroic. After porridge, apple, bread and marmalade, she would have a morning again, and she was not looking much beyond that. That was how she talked, how she explained herself to me.

As I went downhill, feeling the earth tug me, I still felt part of her day, knowing she slept with a long red cord to pull in case she felt ill, and a brace of flashlights, a candle to light with a match from an old-fashioned box of them (book matches she could not manage). The telephone was not far from her, and she had now begun to use it with prudent confidence, once actually dialing the United States and leaving a strained but accurate message on the answering machine. Was she an extraterrestrial transplant of palpable fragility but iron destiny, thus far unrecognized as such and taken for granted as a human? One day she would be gone, but to a spaceship, in which she would regain her normal size and lose eighty years. Many of those who, back in Eckington, had left vegetables or bunches of flowers at her door had never heard her play, or teach harmony and grammar, but their children had. All admired her staying power, most of all her gentleness and

her formal sensitivity. I, being almost an Oriental, doted on
the aged, believing them the most precious repository of life's
blessings. She, Promethean in spirit, had now become an old
lady of the chimney corner, out of some poem by Yeats, except
she no longer had a fireplace to tend, not even a fireplace with
an electric fire mounted in it. Her green-gray eyes had the
abstruse, cleansed look of the seer or the ancient narrator; she
told only of her girlhood, though, and I vowed to organize
myself one year and visit her with tape recorder at the ready,
wanting to get it all down in her own words, as I wished I
could have done with my father's hour-long monologues.
Mothers, she kept telling me, did not expect to watch their
sons age; she giggled, thinking she had affronted me, but she
knew what she was talking about, she who continued by grace
of radar, rote, and something like celestial navigation of the
heart. In her new routine, she would wake at five or six, spend
a penny (as she liked to say, relishing euphemism for its down-
to-earthness), then sleep on until eight or nine, a newborn slug-
abed, listening to the radio until hunger got her up and about.
By eleven she was ready for company, but she knew of old
how late I rose if given a chance, so it would always be somebody else, Rikki or Reyner or my sister, breaking into her
fastness as if each day were a new year. It had all been better,
she told me, in Eckington, when she had had more rooms and
I would sleep under her own roof, be there for breakfast (more
or less), and, especially, be ready for the cricket on TV that
began at eleven or even ten-thirty. There being so few late-late
movies on British TV, I never missed a one, staying up as late
as they ran and being badly hungover the next morning. Her
view was simple: they should not run movies late at night to
tempt me.

The trance of not enough sleep was almost the same as the
trance that used to come with King Arthur. I remembered try-

ing to mellow my performance as I read aloud, smoothing things out, trying to make the lines less end-stopped, at least until a lump in my throat, thrust there by the sadness of beloved things under threat, began to choke off my reading altogether, making me lurch and gasp. It was no use reading Tennyson if it was going to make me emotional while she heard me out with perfect poise untouched by the merest hint of wistfulness, her mind on life, on lines, on the poet, Arthur, Guinevere, the rest of them, her entire response selfless and satisfied; deep down she had convinced herself that any pleasures now, after eighty-five, say, were a surplus, not to be moped about. It was the same when she sang, a little tense to be sure, and her soprano rose clear and convinced against the congregation singing on TV. Then she took the book from me and read the lines herself, a spy exchanging the code word, but bracing herself for the recitation with impassioned dubiety, not sure the words were there on the page, after all, but in her mind only, so there were unassailable question marks after such hefty surds as *thought* and *not* and *fine*. She demonstrated, as a pianist would, how the merest tilt of intonation could unstick an image from its moorings in the poem and release it for an unplanned sortie into the head of anyone passing by. Old enough to quibble, she made a melodrama of the line, marshaling her best elocutional technique to do Tennyson justice without quite neglecting herself. She pleased herself, turning the lines into music that suited her, banishing the poet to Timbuktu. It was possible to say the line "I yearned for warmth and colour, which I found" as if warmth and color weren't worth finding. Through obbligato insinuation of the highest order (worthy of Edith the opera singer, her sister-in-law), she created around the line a diminishing inkblot of lost alternatives, things a Tennyson might well have been expected to think of, and made me think: Well, he looked for warmth and color but found drab Greenland instead. Damn. She called the line into question as, having raised the ghost of its arbitrariness, she made of it something rhythmically superior. Another day, she would say the line even more perversely, leaving me to think that yearning for warmth and color was better than finding them. My experience of hearing my mother read, as she had read to scores of children when she had taught literature, involved me—at least at thirty, say—in transitory states of misgiving, a voluptuous, trusting suspicion that vanished the instant she turned to the next line, never mind how forceful her twistings of it were going to be. Clearly she had gained much more than most from her readings and misreadings of poetry, and I wondered, back when I was a student, what she would make of Yeats, Auden, Eliot, Spender, Gascoyne, but she never read them, sticking to her old favorites like life preservers, as to Bach and Beethoven, Schubert and Brahms. I didn't push things. I had learned from her something vastly important about relativism in literary response. My mother was the first deconstructionist I ever met, a pianistic solo virtuoso who treated literature like a score.

Yet that is too abstract and final-sounding a thing to say about her, much as she deserves it for sheer excellence. I remember keenly, and still want to do it again and again, how we used to take the bus into town and head for a certain bookshop, the most literary of four or five. Heedless of money, my sister, my mother, and I would load up her rectangular shopping basket with books we thought we'd like to buy. What an orgy we intended. How the basket creaked as we took turns to carry it. After the first hour, we began replacing our second favorites, ending up with a book each, over which we pored on the ride back home. As a result we sometimes did not buy the two pounds of best ham we were supposed to get, but took home with us the same weight of pressed "brawn," dotted with nodules of uncompressible fat. These my father would maneuver to the edge of his plate with a betrayed scowl, not that he disliked fat; he just resented the mixed-up nature of this stuff when he had been expecting something lean all through. He never asked us to bring him a book, so he was entitled to complain.

Neighbors

Had I been more hard-boiled (something that three years in the military never taught me), I would not have made a habit of sitting by her chair and leaning against her leg, thinking she was the only person who gave me enough peace with which to withstand the shock of loss. On this one occasion, after listening to some De Falla, she was already asleep, her legs cocked up on the tuffet, her color good, her breathing regular, her stomach for once quiet. No gurgles. No buzzes. This was how it always was when I was over, and I blamed myself for never having been there long enough, for either my father or for her, always gallivanting around the globe on this or that quest. That's how you lose your own life, of course, devoting yourself to your parents, but the Asian (or Italian or Jew) in me suffered and still does for not having been with them enough after a certain age—twenty, say. I had always wanted to protect my mother, and now she had reached ninety-four without me, so perhaps I was redundant after all. It was always too late to protect my father; the damage had been done in France and Belgium.

My morbid mood continued as I reviewed the panoply of all that was to come. People went to funerals eager to see how others bore up under the avalanche of grief; this was where you found samples of uncontained behavior that even the perpetrator had not intended, or guessed might come about. People wanted the insides to come out from under cover, weeping and bawling, roaring and choking, just this once, egged on by all the others present. You could not blame people for wanting to see, in others, how they themselves would look when eviscerated by commonplace disaster, though I do think one or two connoisseurs of intrinsic misery showed up to study the fronts, the skins, the glazes, these being the psychic rain gear of those not emotionally involved, certainly not in the first rank of bereavement. It was pornographic, wasn't it, as with those people who doted on pictures of accidents, executions, and extermination camps. In any society that prided itself on restraint and cover-up, the voyeur is bedrock human, whereas in Bali, Hong Kong, and Delhi it was wholly different, all three poor countries for the kind of novelist who loved to raise the roof and show folk at their trades, in bed, or in the bathroom, tugging the tampon by its string or hoicking the boogie from the nose by tugging at its lowest flake. The novel, I kept telling myself, flourished best in repressed countries like England and Japan, or it used to do so. Or Spain. I hastened away from what promised to be a pointless extrapolation of an average afternoon and put the kettle on.

Yes, I often wore a childlike half-grin on my well-upholstered features, often while planning a chapter or two: the joy was showing through, the demiurgic fascination with being creative simply for the sake of being so, as Mother had taught me—in the old days we had looked at the old masters with something like ferocious envy. And now I was inventing when she was not, something that had not been there before: not children, and not love, but what she had always seen as mystical happenstance, a polished reticulation wafting gently toward her from the heart of the cosmos, coming together in that shape—a ballade or a prelude—because she had willed it into being, that sleek, trembling edifice. That was how her

mind's ear-eye "got" music, how she conceived of the whole,
rather like an aerobatic pilot who, having been allotted a cubic
lump of sky, say five thousand feet in three dimensions, imag-
ines in that box all the maneuvers to be made, as if there were
no other sky. When playing, she visualized chords almost as
silver concertinas, not with studs and grips but as something
fanning out, opening up, then skimming along her arms as she
played. My spine tingled when she told me these things. I had
never realized how close to the visual world a pianist could
be, though I knew how close to music a novelist could be, so
I should have known better. How intense, haphazard, and tan-
gential the thinking of creative people was.

For years, Reyner Rilka and Rikki had been trying to per-
suade her to walk down the hallway as if she were going for
a bag of potatoes, or simply to go around the back to contem-
plate cow or dahlia, and then as it were siphon herself off and
go play the piano in the big comfortable lounge used for bingo
or whist. In other words, a recital. No, she said, rheumatism
had put paid to all that. She had made a special tape for my
sister and me some four years earlier, both playing and talking
about the music (her favorites from Bach to Brahms), and that
would have to do. Frailly intractable, she announced that "Old
ladies of my years should listen, not play." Or something such.
I was supposed, now I was over, to talk her into it, and
vaguely I had tried for four years but always failed, even when
backed up by Rikki, bulky in her velveteen sky-blue jogging
suit, her long nails painted pimpernel red, and Reyner Rilka
(his name gradually contracting under local pressure into
"Rennaril"), ever barefooted in sandals winter and summer,
ever in the old black leather jacket he seemed to have inherited
from a Luftwaffe pilot. He looked much younger than sixty-
two, sixty-three, sixty-four, sixty-five, and his trim gaunt

face reinforced that effect; he seemed eternal, invulnerable, opaque.

Looking at my mother's perfect legs jutting up from the pool of a fallen and unretrieved stocking (life was informal in this building of mixed generations), and marveling at their smooth, unvaricosed solidity, I heard Rikki's pitch all over again: "She's really got rhythm. You can tell that a mile away. Can't you?" Not worth answering. Rikki pronounced her vowels more than the locals did, seeming to gulp for air during them. Now, I wondered, was that Dutch? "I did once," my mother was saying, "but it's all gone now. The knacker's yard for me. I loved to play, but I can't do it anymore. It's done with." She needed the double brandy she used to have, but all she got was Rikki and me seated on the rug on either side of her, pointedly fawning while she gaped at us and yawned, at last announcing that it was time for her biscuit and warm milk, an hour early. Deep down, she was mourning Edith, our coloratura soprano, who had died in the spring, and she grieved as she never had about my father or the some one hundred of her friends who had gone before, including Tranquil Gaunt. I could see how her mind trailed after these dear, spent ones, like Wordsworth in reverse: trailing clouds or skeins of worldliness, they fared away from her, to a kind of abstruse Arizona, where (as I'd told her) the desert was green and in February you could sit outside on a sunny bench and peer up at blue sky through branches laden with lemons. It was seventy degrees all the way from November to April, though chilly at night in a cozy, hospitable way.

"*You* were born in a February," she said, "in a snowdrift. Well, not outside, but the snow had drifted, and my doctor died only the day before." She was misremembering, morbidly embellishing, as she sometimes did, like Mahler. "They all die

the day before," she resumed. "What a panic." Now, as I
recall that afternoon, she once again sat smiling, with Heart
of Midlothian by her holding her hand, or Rikki as they
changed position, with Reyner Rilka standing to attention at
the open door, some flowers under his arm, which he seemed
reluctant to put down, eager not to disturb. She slept and un-
slept; then, desleeped, dozed off again, conquering time with
naps, as if she were watching a movie whose duplicate played
in her head. As her smile wavered and modulated, we were
able to discern her pleasure at least, though not the actual
incidents. The TV was off. Or it was as if she were being read
to by someone whose body was not present, and only genial
circumspection kept her from not telling us about it: we might
not care, we might be bored, we might find it all a bit dated.
She did not have enough hands for us all to hold, so we made
contact with her shoulders and knees, as if these ons and offs
as we swapped positions were the cordial counterparts of the
blackouts or grayouts, ins and outs, that took her away from
us for palpable instants. Who knew what she was hearing?
Perhaps news of cidering and nutting parties in the autumn,
printed sheets of paper dolls from Germany (*Bilderbogen*),
white muslin dresses with sky-blue sashes and real ostrich
plumes for one's hat. Was there still in reverie a world in
which she might ask at the shop counter for Buckingham's
Dye or Savon Helianthis d'Or?

"She's far away today," Rikki observed, looking at Reyner
Rilka, now on his knees, his flowers beside him calling out for
water.

"Traveling," said Heart of Midlothian, sounding envious.

"First class." Rikki.

"She's remembering." Now, who said that?

"Did you ever see such concentration?" Reyner.

"One day," Rikki whispered, breaching a secret, "she'll stay out there. Then she'll come back to take us all with her."

"Shall we be going?" Reyner without his flowers.

My mother's brain was a magic lamp, soft as suet, as fully wired as the wide world's telephones, yet tender with the most fleeting cameo, the slightest vignette, stored away in a whole parade of exquisite instants curled up like moths on a flypaper or dots of Braille on a flexing page. If they ever came through during conversation, as they sometimes did (more often than Mrs. Morgan's lost airman son), you had to drop everything and be their slave, since they were more precious than mashed potatoes, the next sliced pineapple, or God's promises. My mother had acquainted me long ago with the protocol of sudden nostalgia. Things were always coming back to her, hence her sudden spellbound pauses, with memory unearthing chromatic contrasts that reflected the dissonance of Creation entire. No wonder she halted and marveled. There was always, her ecstatic look said, what could be honed to an ever more delightful pitch. Yet, all in all, she could look back on some occasions when flair and impromptu gusto had made her play uniquely, and perhaps that was all that mattered: in the fall, say, inhaling the scent of apples as she went out onto the platform, the vibration of the taxi's motor still in her hands as she began, and the twinge in her bladder that kept her strict throughout. Such components made for performances like no others. She could not have them back (no recording then), but they came to her anyway, assailing and interrupting like shrapnel from a premature swan song. She had melodious handwriting, her son had once told her, and that was because music pervaded her entire being, and she did everything as if it were music—peeling a carrot, watering an impatiens, reading Tennyson aloud. To everything, she felt, you could bring a suitable aesthetic reverence, as she had once said, but the phrase had slid into the open unbeckoned, and she had let it glide away from her, preferring something less glib, such as "a helping hand from poetry."

The dead were as inaccessible as sheet music laid flat under the lid of the piano stool would be to a musical illiterate. My role had been only, after the evening's instruction ended, to sneak into the aspidistra/music room and sniff the aromatic zone where Brenda Levick's or Hetty Green's heated-up hams had sat; puberty had no more raging hunger than that catalytic sniff of antibacterial soap and silky asafetida. At that age we were all dirty little boys, helplessly hunting aphrodisiac. My mother would have believed no such thing.

Now I was again the son who would soon be flying away, so my mother was in fugue, heedless of Heart of Midlothian's patter about *her* son, who went around the world digging canals and being well paid for it. "Ah," I irrelevantly murmured, "a Lesseps with biceps," but on she pounded, her face saying, why, this lovely old woman, both arty and bohemian, was almost too old to have a son of any age. Amazing how they hung on, the children of the very old, still capering about by jet when they might with reasonable cause be extremely ill, far too ill to travel anyway. Heart of Midlothian had sensed a disarray in things; who had been getting more than a fair share of maternal-filial feeling? It was clear she didn't approve. Her face gradually crumpled up as if burning underneath. She preferred what she called the misery quotient in the faces around her to be more blatant. Responsible for both the young and the old, she had had some first-aid training, but she was nobody's nurse, oh no, just a visitor like the Queen, and a relayer of phone calls. She was a humorer at life's feast, but she didn't want her charges to think life wasn't a serious, lethal business, often bleak even at its most productive. Had she been a

Nazi, in an earlier generation, she would have used the term
Menschen-materiel—human stuff—with apposite ease. In her
the Calvinist met the Nazi and the mother the sentimental
Scot. She liked the reason for anything to be solid and familial,
not something airy-fairy having to do with inspiration and a
feeling in the heart as the source of etiquette.

Conceivably, all this pattering around my mother, this laying on of gentle hands, was a means of softening her up, of
getting her to play something not too difficult, not too stuckup. All her life, people had pestered her to play, as if she were
some sideshow entertainer and not, as she saw herself with
tender arrogance, a musical snob. She would not play for just
anybody unless the fit took her; in any case, her gift was not
something you took out and dusted off to suit people and their
aunties; it was a secretive homage to genius. To play pianoforte was to honor the composer: that was all. It had nothing
to do with an audience, not really. It was not social, it was
spiritual, an assignation between two committed souls whose
only mode of communication this was, and usually one-way;
she did not doubt that the composer heard the work played,
but she had no faith in the pianist's ability to divine the composer's absent mind. *It ought to play itself,* she had often said.
Leave the likes of her out of it. Asking my mother to play on
demand was no more sensible than asking her son, the novelist, to tell an anecdote, something at which he did not
excel—he knew no anecdotes and took no pleasure in hearing
them.

Now Rikki, whose comings and goings had been copious
this day, had arrived with something to show, popping across
the hallway in a couple of seconds (half a tick, as Mother said).
Here was—Rikki stopped talking and held her amazing exhibit up to the baked summer light. I saw something that might
have come from Manhattan, something wintry with the Statue

of Liberty being snowed upon every time she shook the vial. But there was no Statue of Liberty in this, though lots of red-flecked snow, and whatever was within lying horizontal. Rikki had had it made up for her in the workshops of the NATO base where she managed the laundries. A little cup of plastic, a compatible base piece, some shavings of white tinted red (though with what I had begun to wonder), and all was complete. What was inside was obvious once she identified it, much shrunken and discolored as it was. "It's Rikki's womb," she said, as if disowning it.

"Her what?" I remember my mother saying, tracking the third person through the enigma. "Rikki's *what?*"

"Remember?" Rikki said, finally willing to laugh. "What did I tell you about going up in jets?" It was almost as if the thing she proffered had come into being the instant she touched down in the two-seater Canberra.

"Well," my mother said. "I'm glad mine stayed where it belonged, though not facing the wrong way as it once did. I do remember their removing my appendix, I think it was, on one occasion. They took something else too, whatever it was. It can't have been my gallbladder. I wonder what they took. I wouldn't want it on my mantelpiece, just to stare at. No fear. Tell me, Rikki, my flower, what do you do with it? Has it *any* uses?" If you hear such things, you remember them forever, even if punctuation has gone to the four winds.

"Beauty." Rikki sighed. "It's not that beautiful, really. It's just a souvenir. You know what the Dutch are like. It's a bit of activity in the old place. No good will come of it now." Rikki again shook the fake snow into circulation and tapped the shell as if to say hello to perhaps the finest part of her. My mother looked away, perhaps having noticed that Rikki was beginning to wind up for one of her impromptu flights of free association, after which, presumably, her funny bone would appear in her lap, felled from eminence. How hard Mother was breathing, as if she had overexerted herself; she was all rales and wheezes after laughing, and I wondered if she needed oxygen. Rikki, whose second name was Wilhelmina, now began to build in midair something so gross I looked away, like my mother. "Even the Nazis," Rikki sighed. "With chloroform."

My mother was already watching TV, switched on as a bolt-hole, engrossed in the maudlin day-to-day doings of a working-class soap called *Coronation Street*, in which everyone was *duck* or *love*. Then she motioned at Rikki and said, "She is my dearest friend," in hyperbolical abruptness, no doubt meaning the only one left alive.

Here they sit, I thought, in a country whose coins weigh you down against high winds because they have abolished most of the paper currency. The pubs have no waiters and you have to fetch your own from the bar. The phones are full of gremlins and frying sounds and some operators address you as Caller, refer you to Trunks, and tell you the number you want is Engaged. Soon the ice cream man's van will come around, its amplified music box playing "Greensleeves." It is a country both soothing and horrendous, with no screens, no air-conditioning, no bright colors. I leave in a week, and how I dread that moment. It takes courage to go from so mothballing a life, so eccentric a peace.

"I'm going to have to be brave later on," Mother was saying. "We all know what for." Her face twisted with drear foreboding.

"I'll be here," Rikki said.

"I'm not very brave," my mother told her.

"But you *are* accustomed to it," Reyner tried. "It's not as if it was the first time." The son felt he was being discussed in his absence, as a blight, a pox, an impetigo.

"It's always the first time for me," my mother said, resolved to spare them no sincerity today.

The son said nothing but felt his blood pressure and blood sugar ascending, his headache start again.

"Or the last," my mother added.

"You never went over with him," Reyner said, tactless to the end.

"*Did* you?" Rikki said, tagging onto the faint, almost ineffable whiff of accusation in the air.

"I never could," my mother said, as she always did. Her boy had always gone off alone to those remote places, like a remittance man, an explorer. Anyway, they were mainly places to come home from. You didn't take seriously anyone who went out there in order not to come back. The serious people were those who went, as it were, on a military posting to foreign parts and resented being away from home, where you came from, where you were born, where you came back to.

"Peel the skin off it," she told me about the salmon. "Charlie Jones got a funny eye from eating fish skin. It affects some people in a strange way." To be sure, I thought, at once wondering if Uncle Charlie Jones, my mother's jolly suitor once upon a time, had ever been part of the Noden clique as they roamed through the woods with my father or played dress-up games in the music room. My father, I imagined, had just stared at my mother-to-be and somehow registered that she was no longer just a person, or a pianist, but a drug, a demon, a lady of the lake, to be dealt with in exaggerated ways that clinched for her the sense of power over him but also tethered her to him in a way that decades later she could never quite pin down despite her grasp of English, her knack for a phrase in a capsule. True enough, I had an enigmatic sense of having been engendered by an incandescent, tumultuous love that never understood itself, by a couple mutually entranced.

Now they were discussing noises off, rock-and-roll music coming from another apartment.

"I don't hear it," my mother was saying, "and I don't feel the vibration. It's not as if it were buses going by."

"From above you's worstest," Rikki said.

"All round's worst," Reyner said. "It would be, wouldn't it?"

"We could always get the police to stop it," my mother reasoned, no doubt wondering why they worried so much about something she had never really heard since her son played his swing records.

"What police?" Rikki stormed on. "They'd be playing the same stuff into their earphones as they pretended to hear you out. The whole world's got St. Vitus's dance from it."

"Well, Rikki," my mother said in her sometimes imperious way, "the only thing to do is to think about something nice and put it behind you. You can't let a small annoyance ruin your day. Sometimes that tree hits the window a hundred times an hour." Sweet reasonableness did not appeal to Rikki, or to me, whose ears were much more sensitive than even Reyner Rilka's. As children, Sheila and I had become accustomed to the sounds of classical piano from ten in the morning, and the sounds had fixed our tastes for life.

Did it help me be specific to say that my mother had kept by her, from her piano-playing years in Market Street to her fourth year in Empingham, a woodwork sliding fire screen, even though she no longer had a fireplace? Or that out of compassion for the toiling embroiderers of Nottingham, Derby, Leicester, Scotland, and Ireland, working sixteen hours daily, she had let most of her whitework go, giving it away here and there because, as she said, "Those girls we never saw were blind by the time they were twenty, like the girls employed in Persia to knot carpets of fine silk."

She sat in a room looking at fields, hearing her favorite music, waiting and wondering. On she sat, looking and waiting and wondering, almost voluptuously reliving her girlhood second by second with a host of "That was when"'s and "He'd no sooner arrived than"'s and "Only a day later"'s. She made memory elastic, opening the pores of time, revealing new pores. On and on she toiled, until all she had to look into was a single pore incapable of expansion, in which her entire life swirled lazily like a top, the spinning colors on its cap the emotions she had felt over ninety-four years, and somewhere in there, cold and underfed in the trenches, was my father, a little boy in a man's uniform: officially clad, hoping that a shell would never land near him or that a sniper would not pot him when he went to the latrine at the back of the trench, only a little cul-de-sac but easier to see into because of trigonometry. Like a little worm curling in a lettuce, he did his business and hurried back to stand on the duckboards that made up the trenches' floors, whereas the firesteps, a foot higher, were of earth only and therefore always sinking. Sometimes, pondering Mother, I found a father I had never known or even heard about.

Try as I did to keep separate what Mother told me from what I imagined for her, I found myself fusing the two, since her first and second childhoods were one. She was ceaseless and complete. Her account of her life came in pieces, but, since she repeated them so often, I soon had the gist assembled of how, fairly recently, Reyner Rilka would station himself at the far end of the hallway and then slowly begin to walk, writhing and hunching, detained by unseen captors. She spoke of this as part of her own girlhood. As Reyner reached Rikki's door, he paused; then the door opened just wide enough to admit him, and Rikki scooped him in. The door sealed itself up again without a sound.

"Like magic," my mother said. "It never fails. The first time, I thought I was dreaming." She could never quite establish if she was in a block of flats or a nursing home. "She seems to drag him in. He never refuses. I've never asked, but I've watched, and it goes on several times a week. I must say, that first time I thought it was a crime of some sort happening. It might have made more sense the other way round, a man dragging a woman in. It's okay, though. Is that how you say it?" It was.

13

‖ THE RAW JOY ‖
OF LIVING

A Good Blood Supply

For a day, I kept watch, squatting on the little soft mat inside the doorway, and then another. On the third day I actually witnessed the event and beckoned to Mother to come and see, especially as Reyner Rilka was walking with eyes closed, setting one foot delicately in front of the other, although nearer Rikki's wall than ours. I could see the line of light that signaled a door opening just a crack, with a human, smack behind it, ready to pounce. I saw it waft open, the arm come out, symbolically as there was no force to it, and Reyner lolled to his left and inward as if he had been counting his steps all the way to the encounter. Then he was gone. Could he have been the womb delivery man? Was he impersonating the rent collector or the milkman, captured for sexual delectation by a brawny, lusty Dutchwoman? What, I asked myself, was their script?

My mother then asked them in for a cup of tea, but they would have popped in anyway, for such was the custom of the building: knock and enter, understandable perhaps in a place as collegial as Flamingo was. I told Rikki and Reyner I had seen them at their game.

"Game?" Rikki's accent was thick as porridge.

"Pulling Reyner into your apartment."

"Oh," Reyner said, "hasn't she told you? Hasn't anyone?"

"His real name," Rikki explained, "is Meyer Bulka. He's a Jew. He used to be French. In 1944 the Nazis found the village school he was hiding in, rounded up the kids, and shipped them to the gas chambers. Some of these kids boarded out with French families." Had she really said this, in English? Where was all this talk coming from? Was I remembering it exactly? Because of the sensational value? "Well," she went on, "when the Nazis were marching them along a certain corridor, a foreign woman, a Madame Lindstrom, slid her door open and beckoned him in. They never missed him, which says a lot about how careful they were being in those days. He likes to live out the escape. It livens him up and makes him think tender thoughts about Madame Lindstrom, who brought him up until he was old enough to think for himself. She was a dry old stick with a dry old stick she sometimes thrashed him with."

Reyner's name wasn't really Meyer Bulka either, my mother said. "Didn't we once know a Lindstrom?" I wondered at the world of appearances, then at the ordinary-looking villagers among whom Mother was living as a transplant. All these people in Flamingo, I then saw, were survivors. Each resident was a flower tended by the rest, blooming surreptitiously in a

soil of the preposterous, by a calm and sedate life giving the
lie to calamitous melodramas left behind. Would my mother,
in some acme of playtime, be one day swept from the hallway
into Rikki's domain, or would she fan Reyner into hers with
a mild beat of her piano-playing hand? I wished my father
were alive to witness such frolicking. Thereafter, when I
walked the full length of the hallway, alone, I involuntarily
walked on the side opposite Rikki's door, lest I be swept away
by—whatever. My mother's friends had histrionic flair,
though there seemed few enough of them; the friends she had
came to her; she did no visiting, hardly able to walk. We hated
ourselves for disturbing her. At the right angle on the right
day, she gave a convincing illusion of being mobile, making
one half-step in this direction, another in that, but only at
enormous cost in breath, which Reyner and Rikki often overlooked. Otherwise she was, as she so often joked, a milk bottle, to be delivered and then returned empty. Mostly empty,
she said, because she mostly had the runs.

Even as I held her warm and striated hands ("a good blood
supply," she'd say, "and a lifetime of soapy water"), I found
myself unable to linger on her girlhood loneliness with only
the piano for company. Forced back into the realm of my own
images, as if Mother had to be seen only in mellow spurts of
lightning, I began to reassure myself that a novelist's role, far
from being uplifting, or choric, or handsome, was to be some
toiler of the night, a night-soil man. And the family chronicler
no better off. The only way to relish leftover lives, I thought,
was to talk to those who had no hope at all, no inkling of
angels and saints and heroes, those who lived their lives like
brushes, scoops, pokers, as cut off from language and its
ephemeral redemptions as the teenager who needs a pop song
to say I love you with.

When I asked her, I got the usual recital of games played,

meat delivered, shirts ironed, sonatas memorized, birds shooed, cats banished, dogs repelled, cows shot, pigs bled, calves malleted, as if the whole world were generic. Long ago she had frozen my father, although in a sentry box of pompous and ungrateful ice; he guarded her world with his blue eyes closed, his hands folded on his chest like a good boy behaving in class; he neither slobbered nor whimpered, neither picked his nose nor pulled the skin off his bottom lip. He did none of his old things, I gathered, and he heard no pianos, neither from Helgoland nor from Taormina, from Madeira nor Odessa. She had brought off, though she never said so, the salvation of his image in the teeth of destruction, like someone protecting a piano by gluing its keys together and planting watercress in the thin soil on top. Thus, with direct mention, we kept the image of my father alive, by fixing on the things he didn't do because he never had the chance.

Rikki's womb had made just about its last flight. My mother dwelt on this notion and laughed a-plenty. I, I came from a country more accustomed by television to watching people's insides, usually peeped at by a tiny camera advancing to the interior through a trocar hole. Only Reyner had not produced something of himself (my mother was her whole body, thinned out by diuretics; I was my pain). One day, he appeared in stocking feet for the first time, responding to some disaster as yet unnoticed by NATO, a *Zeitgeist* as blatant as somebody throwing up on the Queen's lap at a coronation.

After my father's death, Mother stayed on tranquilizers for at least a month and then got ready to meet the American poet with whom her son was involved. Diane charmed her, and we soon went off to London by train, to a sublet apartment in Chiswick that would distract her and give her a nostalgic change of scene (post-Blitz and rebuilt London was a city she did not recognize, however, though she warmed to her memories of it). One day, because she stepped backward at the wrong moment, the doors closed and the Underground train left her behind; we recovered her after some backtracking. She had not budged and, I am sure, would not have for hours. Worse, though, was the movie we took her to, more eager to divert her than to think what we were doing. A devotee of Chaucer, whom she had read as a girl, and laughed with, she was happy to set out for Pasolini's *The Canterbury Tales* and did not seem to notice the chain-reaction fornicatorium the movie was. Why had we taken her to a tup epic? We had no idea, but we had assumed she was one of us. She was. She didn't quite remember Chaucer like that, but it was an entertaining show, she said, hugely polite, though utterly unlike the stuff that she and I used to view at the Electra. I think she was still in shock, and no porn movie was going to awaken her from that grief-struck trance. Clacking away, a metronome might have done so, or James Rushing, Count Basie's "shouter" vocalist, or Rhubarb, the retarded youth who ferried messages throughout Eckington village, misdelivering most, having snited onto them and blurred the address; so he would confront anyone and deliver unto them with forceful mumbled iambs, miscellaneously well-meaning like Reggie Jessup the cobbler, who, to hit, aimed to miss. My mother never referred to *The Canterbury Tales* again, anyone's, and that was her last X-rated movie, perhaps in its heated, perverse fashion an ideal cautery to mourning. Does lust kill grief? I suspect so, but it was as if my mother had had the grieving organ removed from her body, although not her gallbladder, during wet-dream anesthesia. Perhaps, instead of bungling, we did her a favor; but maybe she never even noticed and handed Pasolini the snooze he deserved.

Over the years, as a woman denied and thwarted, my mother took an eager interest in Diane's career as a poet and

natural historian, transposing vicariously, finding it easier to
identify with a woman. There were many things I wanted for
her, not least dozens more pianistic triumphs, fewer pupils,
more concerts to go to, but also, in less strenuous realms, certain rooms of the house I am writing this in: designed, all of
them, by Diane, who inherited her mother's flair for stylish
interiors. So we have, my favorite, a green (or Florida) room
in which exquisite floral tiles conduct the eye upward to a line
of picture windows capped by just as floral green drapes. It is
here that Mother would have propped her feet on a soft has-
sock and observed squirrels, chipmunks, and cardinals from
an observatory outpost comfortable even in winter. This room
used to be a dingy porch with broken screens and stained ceiling until Diane got to work on it, transforming it into some
kind of hanging garden. I often imagine my mother perched
there, on the way to becoming a natural historian herself,
peeping through powerful glasses at creatures new to her,
though often mentioned in letters from her son. Like us, she
would have napped, reduced to a green absent-minded thought
in all that green shade, murmuring an occasional word in
remote-control conversation. Wherever she was (alas, never
here), she contented herself with the vision of a vibrant young
woman pursuing her career without hindrance. The idea of
Diane, a woman of ebullient mind and serious hair, always
gave her a lift. Mildred and Diane adopted each other at a
distance in sisterly tribute, two Libras with birthdays only four
days apart.

Plainchant or Delirium

Now my mother, taking stock of herself as one who had
already devoured time, switched from the present to the safely
embalmed past and had me hang her certificate on the wall,

thus setting up before her mind's eye Sir Hubert Parry, bluff mystic, the Etonian-Oxonian who had signed her parchment on February 18, 1915, whose *Cambridge* and *English* symphonies soon flopped, discouraging him, as she at ninety-four appreciated, from composing further: a Saxon Symphony, a Sherwood Forest Symphony, a Fenland Symphony, a Potteries Symphony, even a Symphony of the Derbyshire Dales. From all such fervent provincialism she recoiled, as a citizen of the realm of Music should. She had even dipped into his lectures, *Style in Musical Art*, but had found the book like chewing nettles. Away with all such pious manufacture, she said, away with cronyism. Just because people were in power didn't mean they were creative geniuses; she had seen the lip service rendered, the obsequious oblivion of the mind that curtseyed and looked the other way; the first-rate, bowing to trash. She wondered that any good music got written at all. Only the renegades, she told me, ever did any good. Among these I did not rank, not musically at any rate. Once again I began to feel guilty about being there at all, of having been born and raised. I took out and stared at my return ticket, on its back emblazoned the airline's numbers around the world. You never have to reconfirm, I thought, not anymore. Nowadays they believe you, at the same time suspecting everyone of smuggling weapons aboard. One phrase in the fine print stopped me cold: "Passengers on a journey involving an ultimate destination or a stop in a country other than the country of origin . . ." made me wonder what an ultimate destination might be, or a stop in a country other than the country of origin. It sounded like a rule from the leaflet that came with a board game—Halma or Snakes and Ladders. Could anyone be sufficiently of a country to go wholly from it? Was not human life a series of charades in which the squirming nonpareil ended up a shy obtrusive, neither belonging nor rejected? Did countries really ever want anyone except as cannon fodder or taxpayers? All the billionaires wanted was millionaires to run things for them. What was this fetish for having millions of witnesses from the lower classes? Did a plutocracy need to be witnessed?

Already I had lost the impulse to read the back of the ticket envelope. Life was like standing outside the room in which a party would begin in fifteen minutes and hearing the ice settling in the ice buckets, with a helpless tinkle, reminding you of what was to come. Perhaps my flight was overbooked, but they rarely fouled up in business class. A family emergency, I could say, and they would believe me because people in business class did not lie, even if they had to be searched for weapons. She, who had last flown in the fifties, was scandalized when she heard about airport security and metal detectors. Airlines weren't worth patronizing, she said, if they didn't know how to treat you properly. I should have kept my mouth shut. Now she was reminiscing about my passion for sad and soggy chocolate cake, about trifles with peeled almonds rigged upright into the cream and the smell of sherry wafting about. I would never eat my greens, she said. Always picky: no crusts, no sprouts, no cabbage, no cauliflower. I was pale because I ate no greens. I still don't care for salads, I told her, after all this time. Nor did I like grass. Salads made me queasy, like the glossy look of eyes behind certain kinds of lenses, as if the sheen of grief had taken over an effect buried in the mineral. Then we remembered the big wooden darning egg in her sewing box, ideal for throwing at a burglar's head. We spoke of my splitting my head open on the school playground, and cutting my knee, leaving a piece of flesh on the asphalt. Then I chopped my left forefinger at woodwork with a three-quarter-inch gouge, and teak dust was my antiseptic. Once, on holiday at the sea, as we returned our rowboat to the jetty, she trapped a knuckle between oar and rowlock, but said nothing so as not to spoil things, she the pianist. A deformed knuckle for life seemed to her a small price to pay for family euphoria. I wince still at the memory; she told and showed us a week later. Had none of us been watching? Did we never look closely at her?

"The one who got really hurt was your daddy."

It almost killed him, I knew. Why had he gone gallivanting off to war at so tender an age, sixteen? What did gallivant mean? To traipse about frivolously, I said, looking it up in the dictionary that was never far away from us when we talked. Perhaps from *gallant* influenced by *Levant*. Where the sun gets up. It also meant consorting frivolously with members of the opposite sex, something your father would never do. Oh no.

"Bless me," she exclaimed, vehement, in a mixed mood. "Won't I miss words when I'm dead!"

If I had had any right to reply, I would have spoken with incandescent crescendo. No, *in* one. Something like heartburn went across the inside of my chest, then sliced downward, an angina of sheer emotion, making me jerk forward as if in some suddenly halting vehicle. I mumbled, I don't remember what, but she failed to hear, still nodding at the exquisite fusion of a gallant with Levant, a beau striding out of the sun toward her, or so I imagined her etymological groping at the caravan, at my father returning from the wars like a crusader, a red cross daubed in blood on his white shield. She was Mildred and he was Alfred, a parallel pair.

"*He* loved words too," she whispered, "as well as monks chanting from the Vatican and German wireless announcers although he could never understand them. They spoke so crisply, he said, as if they meant it."

"Buckshee," I told her. "He liked to say that. It meant free, as in *baksheesh*."

"He also," she added, with a newly nourished smile, "liked

to say *raucous* as *raushuss*. Do you remember? It was no use telling him about it."

"Why," I joshed, "would he ever have wanted to say *raucous* in that quiet house?"

"He meant outsiders. Most of the time, he couldn't hear himself speak for pianos. He loved music, your father did, but he didn't always want to be choked to death with it, he said."

When this free-form dialogue ended, and it repeated itself with slight variations a hundred times, she and I would sit in matching armchairs facing each other and slowly drift into a joint nap of perhaps twenty minutes, heads flung back and arms dangling. It was then, as sometimes in the huge echo tube of a jumbo jet, that I felt I was riding a planet, flung oblivious on its rind as Earth raced twisting. When we came back to life, Mother would make us a cup of tea in her rambling way, which I could never drink and she should not; my substitutes, Roma and Postum, impressed her not at all, and she refused to make them. So I usually ended up making "tea" for us both, a quibbler at life's afternoon frolic.

My mother was flying away from me, receding, fading, victim of some diabolical airline devoted to severance (no return trips). Instead of hungering for the love that hovered on the brink before falling, she shied away into an elegy for all the toys she and my father had showered me with, from the de Havilland Puss Moth, whose rubber motor wound up with the plane still in its box, to the Juneero metal-working outfit that was like a primitive lathe. I yearned to take my mother to movies again, but there was no theater in Empingham. We had held hands at all ages, unselfconscious and unaware of aging, bound by the superior spell on the screen before us: the silver reredos we expected Don Quixote to charge and burst through, horse, lance, and all, out of the shower of orange-peel meteors erupting from behind us. I was beginning to dis-

cover what I called adverse memory, which was memory
reluctant to do its job, as if it had read Proust. This, however,
was not just memory refusing to remember; it was memory
wiping itself out, unwilling to be even involuntary. There were
memories that began and had no end, no elegant terminus.
There were memories spread scattershot over the years,
amounting to no coherent vision of things. There were memories that came out backward, breech memories, and made no
more sense when fondled back to front, like a hermaphrodite
in the dark. There were circular memories of straightforward
events, and memories in silhouette only, memories that merely
murmured a catchword or phrase without identifying themselves further and without yielding themselves up, and visual
memories of aural things, tactile memories of things that used
to smell, and memories that evoked only other memories that
evoked memories even more recondite. Were all these memory
misbehaving or being true to itself for the first time?

Stuff, as I called it, kept coming through from the vast un-
differentiated mass of life lived up, surrendered, shot. I could
no longer sever it from all I imagined. It had all become music,
deprived of local habitation and name. I lived among orchestrated emotions, knowing only planes and angles, pulse
rhythms and extents of headache. I saw my mother's face, its
remnant of a tan, and saw only emotion: not what she had
been through. We had gone beyond history and fable and were
now dithering together in the antechamber of horrors. Did she
ever, I wondered, no longer able to use memory as an instrument of delight, chide me in my teens for sitting at the table
all day, a lovely summer's day, with my nose in a book? Had
it been a Friday? The book sat between fork and fish knife,
the blade all curlicued and engraved, as if fish were not flesh
at all and hardly needed to be cut, had only to be broken and
separated. Then a plate arrived on the open book, the knife

and fork sprang to life, and as soon as I had finished I began reading again, while my mother stood at the open door, wafting it to and fro to rid the house of the fishy aroma. "Get some fresh air," she said. "You look so pale."

Was this a memory, or had I invented it? Was it plainchant or delirium? Words came into mind, answers to questions never put, yet having a quality of unilateral finality I could not reduce to simpler terms. Saying them aloud, I aimed them condignly at the haphazard universe, and they boomeranged back at me, words I had only intercepted. Perhaps they came from propranolol, which made me dream in color, which created in me the eerie peace of the beta-blocker extended as far as inscrutable *trouvailles*. More was rushing through my mind, unsponsored by me, than ever before.

I called the airline and canceled my reservation, but the next day I shrank from that and canceled my cancellation. What could be worse than waiting here in the condemned paradise of my mother's presence, waiting for a worst that might be years away? I had always idolized her, as from an enormous distance, whereas my sister had not. Mother is a symbol of herself, I used to say, and the qualities that compose her. She is a prow. She is the statue of all the energy she has known. Who am I to sum her up? She fades decorously, fumbling with the familiar a bit more each day. Her pains get keener; the supervisor of bodies is trying to see how much she can endure. One wince invades another, and the curse or the exclamation does duty for several. She can't find things. She gets rattled if she even begins to cook. Aromatic in their brown paper wrappers, her *Geographics*, once a treasure trove of Technicolor exotica driving her wanderlust crazy with glossed and glossy yearnings, sit in a neat pile, unopened. She no longer follows sport, and she does not recollect phone calls, letters, cards. Yet she has this wise, attenuated look that reminds you: she has not cooperated in any of this demolition; it has been done to her while she pushed gallantly on, heaving and gasping, with a world war to win. I no longer quite know what she eats or if she has a nose for meat going off. I have caught her with a slice of green bread, at which she has not even looked. It irritates her to have no choice between sleep and scalded stoicism. She wants another year in which we soothe her gums with Popsicles, divert her taste buds with long-forbidden ice cream. When I lift her up from under her shoulders I am brandishing an heirloom doll. I rub her hands to bring the feeling back, and so doing brings it back to mine as well. I cup her forehead with my hand to draw her headache down my wrist into my arm, sapping its electricity: a trick learned from her. I try to ply her with ginger wine, nonalcoholic, but she has lost her taste for it, as for ox tongue, salmon, and fruitcake. Each day, each hour, she seems to be working with less, and Bill, in his prudent, accurate way, has noted that some of the raw joy of living has gone from her even as she paws the air for it, reaching, grasping, feeling something encircle her that will not hold her up. Her face goes dark from time to time. It is late August. She sunbathes no more and flings no ball for the dog. She chugs ahead toward one hundred years with small ripples of misleading laughter, her voice the disciplined creak of an oboe, her smile one of chronic loyal despondency.

I see in her a dun ember I can fan into a glow, mostly with a joke or an outing, some gossip or a Western she does not remember. We tweak her as best we can, but she will not altogether come out of hiding. She does not forgive life for doing this to her. She is quiet, poorly, wan. She sees something I do not, coming closer than ever, and it will ruin her.